Visions

I0099816

Nicholas Alexander Papantoniou

chipmunkapublishing
the mental health publisher

Published by

Chipmunkapublishing

http://www.chipmunkapublishing.com

Copyright © Nicholas Alexander Papantoniou 2013

Cover Illustration by Nicholas Alexander Papantoniou

ISBN   978-1-84991-959-3

Chipmunkapublishing gratefully acknowledge the support of Arts Council England.

Nicholas Alexander Papantoniou

CONTENTS

Visions

Dedicated
To my beloved mother,
Tessa Beatrice Papantoniou nee Gray,
And for my dear father,
Pandelis Papantoniou,
To both of whom-I owe everything,
And for my older brother, Christian,
My best friend.

Visions

INTRODUCTION

Nicholas Alexander Papantoniou, was born in London, on September 29th 1957.

His mother Tessa Beatrice Gray, was English. His father Pandelis Papantoniou, was Greek.

His parents met and married in 1955.

He has one older brother, Christian.

As a child and teen he lived in England, Luxembourg, Cyprus and Greece.

He says he had a wonderfully happy childhood and adolescence.

He and his family were living in Nicosia, Cyprus, during the Turkish invasion of July 20 1974. They stayed on the island throughout the hostilities, although-as British citizens-they were eligible for evacuation.

Nicholas was sixteen, at the time.

He says he was very much influenced, by pop and rock music of the 1960's and 1970's.

Enormously influenced, by Marvel comics, which he read from 1961-1971 and by the films and T.V. shows-particularly American-of the sixties and seventies.

Later on, he was influenced by a voracious reading of history. Predominantly-military history.

As a child, he says he wanted to be a super-hero. In his early teens, he wished to be a comic book artist. He was very good at sports-but never took it up seriously, He also considered being a soldier.

By seventeen, he had decided to become a film director-but he had also begun to be very interested in writing.

In Athens, in mid-September, 1977, after a flash of inspiration on a bus on the way home to Metamorphosis-a suburb of Athens-he wrote his first poem. He was nineteen.

At the age of twenty-nine, during June, 1987, he began to get sudden bursts of inspiration and started writing poetry frequently. An obsessive-compulsive, he noted the time that he began and ended each poem. He writes poetry, usually, in an elated and feverish haste, trying to get it all on paper while the inspiration lasts. Prose-he can write at any time he wishes-but poetry-he only ever writes if and when he feels suddenly inspired. Thematically, he has been drawn to the gothic, the epic, the adventurous, the humorous and the romantic.

His father died in 2002.

After the death of his beloved mother, in 2005, he suffered an extreme guilt/grief reaction.

A year later he was told that he had mild Asperger syndrome in addition to obsessive/ compulsive syndrome.

After the death of his mother, he was bulimic for several years, suffered from a variation of agoraphobia, body dysmorphia, intense psychosomatic fatigue, and a serious sleep disorder.

With the help of occupational therapists, he slowly recovered. He began writing poetry again in 2008 after a pause of over three years.

He is a life-long non smoker, non drinker and non-drug user.

By choice-he has never taken any medication. A fitness fanatic, he exercises, every day. By nature, an optimist, he has lived a life of very considerable isolation. He has written hundreds of poems and many other works. His favourite composer is Beethoven; His favourite poet is Emily Dickinson-although-he says he has never read much poetry. He has many interests and enthusiasms, including Marvel comics of the 1960's, history, films, music, T.V. shows-particularly of the 1960's and 70's, physical fitness, various sports, old-time strongmen and much more. He is single and says he is a 'WCH', White, Christian, Heterosexual.

He says, in 2009 and 2010 he had more flashes of 'inspiration', than ever before.

He sometimes calls them 'visions.'

He has-thus far-very many unfulfilled ambitions-which he would like one day to fulfil.

At the time of writing-that is his hope.

Nicholas Alexander Papantoniou

ACKNOWLEDGEMENTS

Writing poetry was the easy and fun part.
But I owe many people, a tremendous debt of gratitude-for finally getting it all into a book.
Above all, my great thanks, to Linda Whitehead, my former and first occupational therapist, for her patience and kindness and humour, and for helping me hugely, during the most difficult time of my life.
My great thanks also to Sandy Flowerday, my second occupational therapist, for her kindness and patience and humour, for also helping me enormously in troubled times.
My great thanks to Annette Bolderstone-my third occupational therapist-for giving me truly immense help and support, in preparing the manuscript, reading my poetry aloud (A strange experience for me.) and above all, for her humour, patience and kindness.
My great thanks also to Sonia Ahmed, for her absolutely invaluable assistance, in preparing this work on my computer.
My great thanks also to Ravinder Jabbal.
My great thanks to Inês Simão for her quite wonderful assistance in bringing the book to digital completion.
And my great thanks to Andrew Wixon, for his tremendous assistance, with many practical, day to day problems.
And my great thanks also to both Kate Fletcher and Lisa Mortimer-for their encouragement.

N.A.P.

March 24-26 2010

THE HAUNTED HOUSE ON THE HILL
OR A TALE OF AMERICAN GOTHIC

The haunted house on the hill,
Lies just at the end of a long, long lane.
No one in the town-nearby-
Ever speaks of it,
And they never will.
For no one, no one,
Wants to dwell on-
The haunted house on the hill.

For there are rumours,
And whispers and local legends,
That give visiting tourists a chill,
Of things and deeds and facts-
Of weird half-truths and unspeakable acts.
Of doomed, devoted, lovers and suicide pacts,
Which took place, there,
It is said-
On bygone days.

Of fact interwoven with fiction-perhaps,
In a way that-to strangers-mystifies,
Of innocent victims and ghostly cries,
Of mysterious cellars and attics-
Full of gloomy shadows,
And evil men and women who kill,
And the blood they spill,
And things that could
Almost make you ill,
And other stories too ghastly to speak of,
But that happened-
On the haunted house on the hill.

Of children not long ago-
Who used to play there,
Used to dance and sing,
The sunny day, away there,
Just having 'high times',
As they like to say there,
Not so very long ago-
On that haunted house on the hill.

The house is now dusty and deserted-
And has been so for many years.
It holds-maybe-
Too many silent secrets,
Or too many stifled fears,
And is the cause of
Too many sudden tears,
In the town and-beyond.

It stands-solitary,
On the summit of the howling hill-
A dark sentinel.
Within-especially on windy days and nights-
It is full of strange acoustics,
And eerie echoes.
As if the house itself
Has its own old, sweet, nostalgic memories,
And it likes to remember.
And vacant, cobwebby, sinister, silent-
It does remain.

Was it Bobby and Lilly,
Like jack and Jill-
Who went and played-once too often,
By the haunted house on the hill?
Who knows?
But the fields below are empty,
And the children's swings-
On the trees are still.

And there are stories of shrill,
Shrieking, high-pitched screams,
Perhaps-only-some ones, present nightmares,
Or another's, waking, living dreams.
But those are the stories
That the long, slow hours fill,
Of the haunted house on the hill.

There was freckle-faced,
Red-haired, twelve year old,
Hannah van Brock.
An angelic child-by all accounts-
Who one day searching-
For her missing cat, "princess",
Vanished, from the face of the earth.
Or so it seemed...
For all that anyone

Ever found of her-
Or her cat.

There was Wilhelm Herman Huberman,
The local brewer.
A huge, powerful, bull-necked man-
No easy victim.
Known in town, as 'big, old bill'-
Who also vanished,
One late, hot summer night-
On his way home.

There was Mary O'Reilly.
A sweet, delicate, kind and friendly soul,
Famous for her potato salad
With onion, capers and dill,
Who simply disappeared – mysteriously.

There was Anna Lundquist,
And her friend, Joan Middleton,
Who went walking,
One lovely, autumn afternoon-
And were never seen again.

Some say axe!
Some say sledge-hammer.
Some say butchers knife.
Some say poison pill.
Some say the unbelievable.
But it was rumoured that they
All ventured-a little too close,
And-just one time too often-
Near-the haunted house on the hill.

Now is this really all true?
Or just the local gossip swill?
For no one really knows,
Quite for certain-what happened,
In the haunted house on the hill.

One thing-though-few dispute,
For it was in all the local papers
And some beyond.
I was then an ambitious, earnest, young reporter,
Covering the story, for a local paper-so I can refer to it-
With some authority.
Of how a young, happy, newlywed daredevil couple,

Joe and Tina Berossi (nee Pesculani),
24 and 25-from New Jersey,
Once went into the house,
A brief ten minute visit.
For a lark or a laugh or a bet-
For fun-or a thrill.
And they were found, the next day-dead.
In their own hotel honeymoon suite,
In the town-lying-side by side-holding hands-
Fully clothed-on the double bed.
Each had committed suicide,
With a blank-but signed-
Suicide note, under a paper-weight,
On the window sill.
No one ever found out why.
But how the speculation did fly!
Wondering and weaving, towering tales-
Of the haunted house on the hill!

It's such an American story!
Of God-fearing, plain-speaking folk.
With guns and home-made apple pie,
And a small town, mid-west culture,
And a flag-so proudly on the porch.
It's such a beautiful, natural,
Wholesome place-so it seems-
And the music has such a strangely inviting trill,
And a Church and a parish that-
Perhaps-knew a little too much-
Of the haunted house on the hill?

It's a place where people,
Young, middle-aged and old,
Do strangely disappear.
It's a place that is filled-so very much-
With, 'Hush' and, 'Shush', and fear.
It's a place, where, from every point,
Looking slightly up,
You can see an old building near,
And it captures your attention,
And causes you to peer.
There are so mad or crazy stories,
Each with a flourish-or a truth-or a frill.
But you can never get at the truth,
No matter how you bribe,
No matter how you grill,
No matter how you drill,

You can ask and ask
And ask and ask.
But the results are always nil,
Since no one wishes
To comment upon-
The haunted house on the hill.

But they whisper-
Mad horrors, were once committed-
With a supernatural skill,
And that nameless, unknowable
Things-did live and dwell-
Inside-
The haunted house on the hill.

For there are tales of hushed, soft, silky moans
And old, cold, lonely bones, that in the meadows lie.
But you can never find out, precisely-what's true,
No matter how hard you try.

Yet-no reporter from anywhere,
Can dig his spade in soil
Down deep enough,
To uncover-though what he digs up-
It may-well make him shudder-
And the hairs on the back
Of his neck stand up.
And the truth will never be known,
At last-until,
Someone opens
The huge, old, creaking, wooden door,
On the haunted house on the hill.

For the chill October wind, blows leaves down the lane,
And Halloween is on the way,
And there are things, that make you doubt if you are sane,
On a beautiful sunlit day.

So, my advice to you is-stranger-
Please-stay, stay away-by now-I think-
You should know the drill.
Whatever you do, don't-
Go anywhere near,
The haunted house on the hill!

You ask-
How long has this been going on?
The answer is-no one knows for sure.
Some say since five and twenty years ago,
Others say-since people were writing with a quill.
Still-no one-here-asks too many questions about,
This haunted house on the hill.

The tales of dried blood,
And chopped body parts,
Of Patricide, Matricide, Infanticide too.
Of witches covens and black mass, of Satanism,
Or devil-cults and pagan, heathen ways,
To me and you-of wild, mad, sexual orgies,
Of beautiful, naive, women and trusting men.
And innocent, children captured.
Of unwilling victims and unholy-screaming-séances.
And incantations and demoniac ceremonies,
And blasphemous, malignant, invocations.
Of jealousy and envy and hate and rage.
And human ghouls and terrible curses.
Of ghosts of murderers and murdered.
Of a madness said to have afflicted
Anyone and everyone-that ever lived there.
Of cannibalism, witchcraft and necrophilia,
And ritual abominations.
Of poison and dead, bold, inquisitive preachers,
Bodies burned after ritual murder.
Of devil-worship and dark sacrifice.
And beings who delight in evil.
Of ghastly rites and malevolent cults,
And gory, gory, stomach-churning stories.
Of shouts, words and doomed deeds-still-and ever to be-unknown.
And terrible screams for help, hollow laughter
And lamentations of despair-
Drifting far, far away-on the late night winds.
And other things-too revolting to speak of-
Too unimaginable-to even contemplate.
And said to have occurred-over years-and decades-
If not-over the turning centuries-
On a haunted house on a hill.

Is this nonsense?
Superstition?
Folklore?
Local myth?

Simple, homespun, credulity?
Who can say-for a fact?
I look up at the house-
And ponder and wonder.

It's the house-some whisper-
That makes-all its dwellers-utterly mad.
It's the house-itself-that's evil, distorted, foul and bad.
And thinking of all its victims
Will only make you very sad.
And turning and leaving it far behind you-
Will always make you very glad!

Yet how can I tell?
On such a glorious day-
On such a lovely, autumn day, like today,
Clear blue sky-bright sunlight-
It's all so utterly impossible to believe!

But something tells me-
As I look into the beautiful blue,
Something tells me-and it might also tell you,
As it tells other believers,
And there are few-
That all the rumours are true!

For the missing children-
The adults too-
Were never, ever found.
And little-and grown up-
Unidentified, bones were discovered
Not so far away-in the ground,
And at night many have heard-
On gusts of breeze, a muffled-
Sobbing and childish sound,
Where no child has played,
For many years and years!

So if it's alright with you my gentle soul,
I have spoken of some of this-but not the whole,
And now I can hear the local church bell,
Starting to toll.
It's getting late-it's getting late.
It's getting dark-it's getting dark.
So I think-I think-
I'll now-just be going on my way.

These are things-these are things-
That may be mad-that may be bad-
That make me sad-
But that make me glad-that
I'm a simple, God-fearing,
And righteous American man.
I don't do everything right-
But I do everything right-that I can.
My ancestors were puritans,
And deep down-deep down,
That's what I am!

For someone must battle-for the fading light.
And someone must strive-against the growing darkness.
If we don't fight for the good-on this earth,
We too-one day-will face the oncoming starkness.
If we don't fight-with heart and soul-for our heaven,
We will surely face-one day-the hell of the heartless.

God help us.

The haunted house on the hill,
Lies just at the end of a long, long lane.
No one in the town-nearby-
Ever speaks of it,
And they never will.
For no one, no one,
Wants to dwell on-
The haunted house on the hill.

August 22 2010   2.10-2.22 a.m.

THE CORE OF LOVE

When I float, when I dance, when I sing, when I hum,
And when I soar with love.
I touch the core of love.

As I hear the melody, the harmony, the syncopation, the whisper,
And the roar of love.
And I touch the core of love!

With the I do, I will, I must, I want,
And I adore of love.
I touch the core of love.

In the longing, the passion, the pain, the ecstasy,
And the gore of love.
I know, I touch the core of love.

With the more and more and more and more,
And more of love.
I touch the core of love.

In the guilt, the innocence, the justice, the glory,
And the law of love.
At once, I touch the core of love.

And in every atom, and soul, and heart, and spirit,
And pore of love.
I touched the core of love.

In how it hurt, it cut, it ached, it throbbed,
And it tore with love.
Even then, I touched the core of love.

And in the peace, the truce, the victory, the defeat,
And the war of love.
Still, I touched the core of love.

In the labour, the loyalty, the fatigue, the repetition,
And the chore of love.
Yet, I touched the core of love.

Nicholas Alexander Papantoniou

On the water, the ocean, the sea, the beach,
And the shore of love.
Oh how, I touched the core of love!

And when you raved and cooed and promised and trusted,
And swore of love.
It was then-I touched the core of love.

September. 15. 2009

THE PRINCESS OF PEANUT BUTTER
Or AN AMERICAN FAIRY TALE

The princess of peanut butter was beautiful,
A princess-real and true!
To be true, to be kind-to do always good,
Was all she wished to do!

Her hair was blond, her eyes were blue,
Her lovely face bore a glorious smile!
To help and give and save and love,
Without cunning-without guile-

Was all that she could do,
And that was what she did!
In sympathy and empathy for all,
No thought was ever hid-

By her-to comfort all who needed-
In open, loving, gentle ways.
To bandage those, who bleeded,
Was how she wished her days-

To be-no one was free from her help and love-
Who needed it-or her kind ways and touch!
No mortal being-no one-I think,
Had ever loved so much!

The peace she gave-the comfort she sent-
Would not be believed-in truth-
Had we not all seen it, with our own eyes,
And realized-all it meant.

The empress of peanut essence!
Radiantly dressed, in blue and white,
Reached for the forlorn, the downtrodden, the helpless,
It was a wonderful sight-

To see-and eloquence must be heard!
But all that was heard-from others-was a stutter.
The only fluent, soaring words,
Were from the princess of peanut butter!

Beauty and truth shone with light!
In every word she did utter.
And many who listened-followed-
The princess of peanut butter!

She spreads herself so thick!
Her dreams are dreams for all!
Her goals are goals for everyone!
Her faith can never fall!

But her friends are far and slow!
And her enemies dwell deep in a gutter.
It makes you want to weep!
For the princess of peanut butter.

But her-fate might yet-be chunky or smooth-
As her enemies plot and sputter,
For a love that knew no end-was the love-
Of the princess of peanut butter!

She needs allies, she needs loyalty, she needs help!
But her friends all dither and putter-
It could make a statue yelp!
For the princess of peanut butter.

Her vision was of grace, of hope, of wonders most sublime!
But they closed her vision-with an iron shutter,
And where else could you climb,
Good princess of peanut butter?

Her foes were all well organised!
Her friends were in a clutter.
For victory is very highly prized!
Graceful princess of peanut butter.

Oh, princess, princess most beautiful and true!
You face the blade-the cold flesh cutter!
Do save yourself while you can!
Oh, my princess of peanut butter!

Run my princess-go-I beg you!
You cannot die-you must not die!
For I-my princess-cannot protect you!
But she was too good-and too brave-to fly.

How they lied and tricked and then deceived,
How they did cluster, bluster and splutter!
To trap the noblest, gentlest woman that lived-
The princess of peanut butter!

There was many a vain and vapid poser,
And many a sanctimonious strutter!
But none risked a finger to try and save-
The princess of peanut butter.

There was many a lachrymose lamenter,
And many a tentative tut-tuter!
None lifted a hand or foot-to help rescue-
The princess of peanut butter.

I tried to force her, I tried to make her-
But she would not, would not, would not go!
What goodness and sweetness and love she had-
They will never, never, never, know!

And so they killed her, ah, the cowards, the hoards.
I could not stop them-I tried-God knows!
My beautiful princess was calm, serene,
Until-the very end.

She was too good-too good-for this world-
And the world repaid-as the world always does.
I cannot get over it-I never will-
Oh, my princess, I loved you so!

If I could have died to save you,
Gladly-I would-but I couldn't.
I could not save you-from your own goodness.
For you could not ever be-less than you were!

And who will say a prayer,
For the princess of peanut butter?
Who makes the bosom heave with joy,
Who makes the stomach flutter?

And who will chant a hymn,
To the queen of peanut cream?
Who makes the love-rise to the surface-
Who makes the spirit beam?

Who brought life and truth in the gold-pink sunset!
And happiness in a flood!
For the noble woman of human kindness?
For the nurturing mother of milk and blood?

And who will sing a requiem.
For the princess that we lost?
Who gave and saved and loved and healed,
And never cared the cost?

But no one, no one did.
They turn away, they walk away,
They shake their heads and mutter.
And though she gave all she had,
They abandoned her,
The princess of peanut butter.

June.20. 2.40-3.15.a.m. 2010.

FLYING TEENAGE GIRLS

Heather was thirteen,
A green-eyed, red-haired, pale-faced girl.
I saw her once-once long ago,
She was so pretty, sweet and sad-
Where did she go?

Susan was fourteen,
A brown-eyed, brown-haired, pink-faced girl.
I loved her once-but never told-
When I was young,
She was so beautiful, merry and bold-
Why did it ever fold?

Anne was fifteen,
A hazel-eyed, dark-haired, pallid-faced girl.
I smiled at her-just passing by,
When a mere youth,
She was so lovely, winsome and shy.
But she did die.

Sharon was sixteen,
A blonde-haired, blue-eyed, freckled girl.
She won my heart-when I was a teen,
She was so gorgeous, wild and free-
Her face-it always stayed with me.

Karen was seventeen,
A chestnut-haired, grey-eyed, milk-faced girl.
She spoke to me-to my surprise,
A single time-when I too was 17,
The path to joy was in her eyes-
And what did it mean?

I feel that they must still exist,
As perpetual, everlasting, teenagers.
Floating or flying in timeless space,
As they so richly deserve to-
For the calibre of their innocence and hope,
And the poignant truth,
Of their ephemeral loveliness,
Sweetness and new-dawn beauty.
Or for the strange assonance,
Of the remembered moment when I saw them,

Knew them-understood them each.
And for the brief glow,
They gave to the world.
To this evil and wicked and beautiful,
Wonderful, transcendent world.

Heather, Susan, Anne, Sharon, Karen.
Thirteen, fourteen, fifteen, sixteen, seventeen.
You're teenagers, forever.
And I am too, with you.

Dancing on orange-pink, sunset, clouds.
Or in the silver-blue, moonlit, summer skies.
With such infinite teens delight.
It was the best light of living,
That I loved,
And you loved too.

And that-I think-
Is the way that it should be.

Still-when I think of all those and other,
Beautiful-departed, teenage girls.
Of yesterday, today and tomorrow-
To me-it seems such an awful,
And terrible crime.

For they never, never learn,
That you cannot earn,
The slightest boon-
From time.

October 11 1989   9.15-9.40.p.m.

SONG OF SUSAN

My name is Susan,
And I've been beyond, the grave.
To spooky, twilight places,
Where skinny, shadows rave.

You would not believe all
The weird things I have seen,
Just me-a flaky, freckled,
Bitter-sweet seventeen.

Once upon a time-
I was in a horizon of gloom,
And I said to myself:
"Over there is an ancient tomb."

Around me were many spirits,
Ghouls, werewolves and things-
A group of anorexic vampires,
With semi-transparent wings.

In a translucent twilight they
All whispered words most foul-
And I found myself-
Staring-at an owl.

I was in a hall-with no way out-
But above-two open doors.
So I cried and I wept:
"No more, no more, no more."

I couldn't believe all I was seeing,
Being human a human being.
"If only I can go out," I thought,
"Before those two doors close."
And I rose is a rose
Is a rose as I rose.

Once out of that hall,
I was in a larger yet,
"This is the beginning of
A mysterious journey I bet!"

Nicholas Alexander Papantoniou

I observed-a shadowy figure-
Moving across the light,
And my ears and my eyes and
My soul jumped in fright!

So I swallowed my rejoicings,
And all my flippant boast's-
I saw rows is a rows
Is a rows of waiting ghosts.

One danced and spoke in whispers,
And asked me to dance along.
And I danced and I danced,
And I danced and sang a song.

I saw a ghost covered in blood,
As though attacked by a lethal mugger-
But I knew in my secret soul-
He was just a rotten bugger.

I saw a song shaped like a school friend-
But I don't remember which.
I said:"Song-who are you?"
She said: "I'm the song of a bitch!"

I saw a strange landscape-
I walked across diagonally,
I was out-I was free-
"Liberty, your name is me!"

I saw a girl in a mirror,
The opposite of myself.
I watched in fascination,
Then walked boldly past the twelfth-
Of all the dozen mirrors-I passed-
And each was very true,
But in reflecting mirrors,
I saw nothing new.

A horizontal woman-she-
I-the vertical,
My soul and body are radiant,
But not symmetrical.

I found an oarsman-sitting in a boat-
The boat was outside the castle-
Lying in a moat.
I jumped in behind him.
I said:"Row for Heaven's sake!"
And he rows is a rows
Is a rows across the lake.

Never can I tell this to
All my snotty peers.
And face their envy, their laughter
And all their snotty sneers.

Perpetual I advance,
Advance I perpetual.
Peripheral all else,
All else peripheral.

To many people material things
Are rather delectable,
But my idea of heaven-
Is purely conceptual.

My mind like my memory,
Is easily stimulated.
And I think in rapids streams
Of things, I've loved and hated.

My imagination-like a tower-
I don't have-
Is easily erected.

My hope-like a bridge-
You don't have-
Loves to be connected-

With all the light,
And all the glory,
That dwells in the universe.
I say:"life is sometimes painful,
But joy always comes first!"

My faith-like my optimism-
Easily protrudes.
When it is touched by wonder-
And all that this includes.

I left the castle.
The lake then took me home-
And instead of monstrous figures-
I saw many a curious gnome.

A circle-360 degrees-I've come,
And gone-and now I'm back.
I've filled in many gaps I had-
And I no longer lack.

Only a mist separated me,
From all I wished to gain-
I found victory on the ground,
Where defeat before-had lain.

I know the immortal spirit,
That dwells in you!
That dwells in me!
So I flew through
The darkness to light-
And clasped my liberty!

April.14.1989

THE ELF–PRINCE

The horseman rode upon his way-
And could not cease until the day.
The heart of his love-he bore in his hand,
His love lay waiting, across the land,
Until her heart was laid to rest,
Again in its home-within her breast.
For it was taken-that he would know,
Her heart would shield him from his foe.
The elf-prince-would not let him through,
Until shown a heart-that was faithful and true.
She said:"Then take my heart-but bring it back-
Before morning comes-or I die for the lack.
Remember my blood-that stills for your sake,
I'll wait for you my dearest-here by the lake!
Then do hasten to return-O my valiant lord-
But defend yourself from evil with your sword."
She with hair of crimson and eyes azure,
With a will so firm-and a heart so pure.
He said;"There is no danger-I would not meet,
There can be no menace-I cannot defeat."
"If morning comes," said she "and I am dead.
For your betrayal, my eyes will turn red.
If dawn arrives-but comes without you-
My flesh will whiten-my hair will turn blue."
He kissed her hand so strong-but now so pale
And rode his great black horse-over hedge and hill and dale.

He rode so fast the trees did seem to burn!
But his soul did tremble and his heart did yearn.
Into the forest-with his true loves bond.
He saw the elf-prince, standing beyond.
He knew indeed-he had fulfilled half the course,
He looked at the awful prince and reigned his horse.

Upon the heart-the Elf-prince did peer-
His eyes did narrow and he did sneer:
"You are for truth, a very lucky man!
For most are abandoned and weep as they can.
For them there is no faithful heart-they see their error,
They moan in pain and shake with terror!
Their tongues then stiffen-their blood will freeze-
I take their hearts and turn them into trees!
The men who died-their spirits are not seen-

Nicholas Alexander Papantoniou

They cover the earth in leaves of brilliant green!
Get you away-and never dare cross my path again
Or I will have your heart-as I do all other men!"

The horseman rode on to his waiting love-
"What happens now-is in the hands of one above!
I must reach her before morning-O God-I must!
I cannot betray such a wonderful trust!"
His horse was weary, foamed and snorted in pain,
Yet its hooves did gallop with a thunder-naught could tame.

He reached-at last-his true loves spot-
His heart was pounding and his brow was hot.
The sun was rising-behind the wood,
On a day he would remember-for evil or good.
"Now, I will see if our faith was justified!
Will she be living-or will she have died?"
He found his true love on the ground.
She made no movement-uttered no sound-
He put back the loyal heart that she did give,
She opened her eyes and she did live.

May 24 1995   8.10-8.34. p.m.

THE SHAPE OF LOVE

I am the round,
You are the square,
I don't look for corners,
They are your lair.

I am the circle,
You are the rectangle,
My circumference is smooth,
Your edges can mangle.

I am the oval,
You are the triangle,
I love my cool perimeter,
More than your hot tangle.

I am the helix,
You are the pentagon,
I hold no surprise,
Your form is a con.

Love is about angles and curves,
Temporal and eternal,
With straight lines and swerves-
Infinity blossoms to a function.

Life is immortal-
Spreading into hope,
Dissolving into spirit,
When matter cannot cope.

Love is a shape,
But our shapes-cannot be.
Life is a kinetic joy,
Of spatial liberty.

How to love-
How to love and remain free?
That is the most puzzling question-
Of life's, geometry.

Nicholas Alexander Papantoniou

October 6-9 1989

THE NIGHT RIDER

In old Germany,
There is a ghostly fiend,
And he rides by night.
Many on roads and fields have seen him,
It is a dreadful sight!
When he gallops past,
All travellers hide-
And hold their breath.
For his great, white horse
Is the colour of death.
Himself, has a deathly pallor,
With glowing, gothic,
Red and green eyes.
No man-of whatever valour-
Can evade-his mortal surprise.

A young and simple girl,
Is walking through the wood.
She is not in bed, in her village-
Sleeping-as she should.
Scanning the night and woods
The rider sees her figure.
He turns his horse,
And gathers himself,
As finger on a trigger.
The girl goes on all innocent,
Of what lies close at hand.
She is on her way to her house-
Fifteen miles across the land.
Unknowing and un-fearing,
Upon, her moonlit walk.
With a grunt of anticipation,
The night rider begins to stalk.

'Once I followed a bird and I knew where he flew,
As he followed the sun-so I will follow you.
As close as a mother-my child-you are to me.
We will be one in spirit-eternally.
You cannot escape me my angel, my sweet!
 I do echo the rainbow of your flying feet!
Not too high-nor too dizzy-upwards can you soar!
Nor plunge too deep under the oceans timeless roar.
Your heaven-blue eyes and golden hair-have called me!

Your maiden's limbs and chaste spirit-enthralled me!
Your virgin charms-your pure white arms-have won me!
Ach! Foolish, foolish, foolish girl-to shun me!
The earth resounds-with woodland sounds-as I pursue thee!
Your naked feet-on moss or wheat-are ever closer to me!
You listen, to my horse-thudding, thudding, through the trees!
I listen, to your sobbing, sobbing, gasps and pleas!
No forest can hide you, from my luminous gaze,
For I tell your heavenly scent-in a thousand ways!
My eyes search all the woods-they glow green in the dark,
Your figure is exposed to me-always-distinct and stark.
Your headlong body-reveals me-where you roam,
In the middle of the forest-but thou and I alone!
Many leagues from refuge and none shall know your screams.
My girl-they cannot hear you-within the world of dreams!
Flee forever-still-I would follow thy trail-
Still-you would hear my pounding hooves,
And I see your face so young and pale!
I will reach you in an instant-
And you will feel my touch-
Within your ribs-a hand of ice!
Your soul is worth so much!'

But-what is this?
The rider slows,
His horse begins to falter,
That iron, Teutonic will of his
No obstacle can alter.
And when it seems-triumph he must-
His resolution turns to dust.
Now the pounding fades!
Now the snorting stops.
Now his joy is frozen.
Now his frenzy drops.
Naught else-but this could save her,
Or the rider lets none go by.
And the fury leaves his blood.
And his ardour swift-grows shy.

The night rider cannot take them-
Be they saint or be they sinner.
The girl smiles at him-and waves fond farewell!
She ate garlic for her dinner.

September 15   2010   3.12-3.15.a.m.

THE ETERNAL ECHO

A good deed is a soaring dove,
A bad deed is a crawling gecko,
For every good and evil deed,
There is an eternal echo.

Is your life full of lofting birds,
Or dense with creeping lizards?
Ask yourself this O man or woman,
As you face life's moral blizzard.

October   20-24   1989

THE BRIDE ROBBER

Hans and Gerta,
Married in joy,
And went to a nearby village,
In Germany's, wooded lands
That once was pillaged-
In the seven years war,
Beyond-the touch of reason or law.

The newlyweds,
Moved into the house
They liked most.
They did not know-
Within-dwelled a ghost!

The spirit of a man-it is said-
Whose wife-was killed-
By soldiers-on their wedding night.
Many men and women of the town
Had seen him-
It was a hideous sight.

Loving and beloved,
Yet robbed-of his bride-
The wretched man-that night,
Became a suicide.

Now he haunts the town-
And any new wed girls,
With entreaties and enticements-
His spirit about them swirls.

And many times the newlyweds,
Do flee in horrid fear!
In case his ghostly form-
Again to them-appear.

The woman-Gerta-waited-
In the brides room,
While Hans-her man-changed.
She heard a growing sound-
That she thought was
Something strange.
'It cannot be a horse, nor a dog,

Nor yet a bird,
And yet, I am sure, I heard
Some faintly whispered, word.'
She thought.

Then in the dark,
She saw a tall, thin figure slowly appear!
In ghostly, shining blue,
With glowing, luminous, staring, eyes.
She stifled a scream.
Her scalp did stir.
Her heart was pounding too.
The ghost spoke-
In whispered, haunting tones;
"Come, with me O wonderful woman!
Thou excellent woman and maid,
I will worship your body and soul,
You need not be afraid!
You have a beauty-nothing can dim,
Quintessence of the feminine-
You belong to me and not to him!
So come, into my heart and soul O come!"

"Oh, please, Herr Spirit,
Choose another maid!"
Said Gerta.

"No! No! I must have you!
For soon the night will fade!
And so will I!"
Said, the ghost.

"My wife was like you,
Blue of eye,
And blond of hair,
And was it right?
And was it fair?
That I should lose her
Before we were one?"
Gerta-did not reply.

The ghost moved closer to the maid,
And spoke in louder tones-more urgent-
And pleading.

"Come hither-delicious maiden!
I'll hold you close to my breast,
I wish to know your soul,
Before the moon goes west!
Let me plunge within you,
And ride you like a storm!
The night is clear and cold,
And I must keep you warm!"

Gerta said nothing.
She was struck dumb with fear,
As his voice again echoed in the room-
As though, from far beyond!

"Come with me O wonderful creature!
Thou beautiful, glorious, Jungfrau!
I will treasure your every feature,
If you will come with me now!"

"Come, break the spell I'm under!
I will show you a wonder!
I wish your soul to plunder!
Come, O beautiful bride!"

"Come with me O thou divinity!
Come with me and roam infinity!
You will know of all sublimity!
If you come to me-now!"

The eyes of the ghost,
Glowed, deep blue-in the dark.

"Do not now be hesitant!
Your hand is mine to take!
We will be forever one,
Ere, by the dawn we wake!
We will live together,
Forever in happy times!
We will watch out children grow-
And hark! The bell now chimes!"

Gerta screamed and ran from the house-
Just as the church bell was chiming.
Hans, called out her name,
And into the bride's room he went
And there he stood,
And watched and listened and paled,

Till all his courage was spent.

He saw the ghost,
In ghostly light,
A-dripping ghostly, purple, blood.
He saw a corpse emerge,
And ghostly garments don.
He saw the hollow, staring, eyes,
He saw a skeleton.
He saw the drunken soldiers,
Their swords, were running through
The helpless, screaming woman's body-
Her brides dress white and new.
He saw her stained with crimson,
He saw the soldiers leave,
He saw a man beside her, kneeling-
He saw his bosom heave.
He saw his hands coated
In his brides warm blood-
He saw the figure open the window
And leap.
The candle went out.

Gerta thought herself deluded,
And returned to the house.
And climbed the stairs,
Treading like a mouse.
She entered the room.
There was nothing strange, within.
'I must have fallen asleep,
And dreamed it!'
She thought.

She lit another candle,
She called out "Hans?"
And approached the bed,
She touched his face.
Her husband was dead.

October 13   2011   3.46-3.48. a.m.

EYEBROWS

I browse through infinity,
With the power of my mind.

Eyebrows will be raised-
At what I might find.

I browse through time and space,
In search for immortality.

Eyebrows above my eyes,
For all eternity.

August.16.-19.1992

THE CASTLE BY THE SEA

The rich handsome lord,
Received two parcels,
The rich, mad Lord,
Who lived in the castle,
The rich, young Lord,
Walked the cliffs eternally-
And lived with his mistress,
In the castle by the sea.

That is the legend,
That has past down the years,
To encourage the faithful,
And give the pliant fears.

The castle was old,
And its Lord was great.
With every blessing,
Endowed by fate.

The castle rose grand,
On a cliff by the sea.
On a noble prospect,
Both to you and to me.

The castle stood tall,
In the amber-pink gloaming.
Above the blue-silver waves,
Forever, crashing and foaming,
Against the dark grey rocks-
As the seagulls, soared above.

While the timeless, oceans,
Surge and toil-
Upon old England's,
True and sacred soil.

In the village they whisper,
And shake their heads,
And it is a great lesson,
To all newlyweds.

A piece of life,
That points to a moral!
To young and old lovers-
Who love and quarrel.

Now, this Lord was very handsome,
And his heart was too free.
He married a woman for her wealth and family.
A woman of rank, of high birth and standing,
With a character-hard, proud and commanding.
A woman much older-and in truth-rather plain,
So perhaps some matchmaker-deserved of the blame.
For the wife was demanding and the wife was jealous,
She watched her husband with an eye both sharp and zealous.
Her husband grew weary of her fading charms,
And his eyes looked for pleasure-in another woman's arms.
He found a woman-young, free-of wonderful beauty-
Who had no inkling of rules nor duty,
That bind a man-when he takes his vows,
And bows to both matrimony and to spouse.
She was charming, she was giddy-she was kind and sweet.
And with her on many evenings-her young Lord did meet.
They spoke of their love-of their passion and longing-
Of all the joys-that are in the world thronging.
The girl was modest and chaste and pure.
And would not give herself-until she was sure.
'As I love you,' she said, 'So you must love me!
And we cannot-and will not be together-until you are free.'
And he did truly love-his mistress so fair.
And began to dream of a life they could share.
He formed a plan but does him-no credit,
Though unto his mistress-he did not tell it.

He poisoned his wife-but the poison worked slowly.
In a day she was ill and very lowly.
In two days-she was dying-but did not guess the truth,
Though several times-she cursed the looks and youth,
Of a young and happy girl-whom her husband often spoke with,
After three days-her life-she nearly broke with.
But still had the strength to walk the castle ramparts high,
And thought of her life-with a shudder and a sigh.
She paced the grey stone and looked at the tumultuous sea,
On a noble prospect-both for you and for me.
She thought of her life-with sorrow-but no fears,
And as she gazed at the raging sea-her eyes filled with tears.

Then looking-later-in an old cupboard-
She found the poison phial.
She saw a plot-
Both wicked and vile.
Her mind did fill-
With fury and rage.
Made worse by her illness,
And her age.

A warning to lovers,
To cover their tracks.
The wife had a pistol,
A knife-and an axe.
The jealous, aging wife-
Who had learned the facts.

She was taken to her cottage,
In the nearest town.
For she said-there-she could
Die content-without a frown.

She asked the mistress,
To see her-in secret-that day.
Before her body,
Was laid-in the grave.

The mistress went-she was true-without guile-
And the wife did meet her with a smile.
The mistress knew nothing-of the poison plan,
She only knew that she loved a man.

The wife used her pistol,
And just had the strength-
To use the axe and knife,
Though it took some length.
At last she had done it all-
All without a sigh.
She got into bed,
And she did die.

The Lord learned of his wife's, death.
She was laid in the ground.
Although the mistress-
Could not be found.

The Lord awoke, next morning,
Full of joy and glory.
His life would begin,
A fresh new story.
With his mistress, he now
Would live and marry
And no more than a month,
Would he tarry.

For he knew-soon-
His mistress, would return.
And the now-free-Lord,
Did long and he did yearn.

The next day,
Two parcels arrived.
He opened the smaller one,
Curious and surprised.
He unwrapped it,
And then stood still
And with silence the room
Began to fill.
He let out a shriek,
But never a word he said.
Inside the parcel,
Was his mistress's, head.
In the other parcel,
Wrapped in garments,
Blood stained, foul and shoddy,
He opened and found
His mistress's quartered body.
And with it-wrapped in paper-
Like a quiet, hidden, wink and a smile-
He found the half empty, poison phial.

A lesson of what happens,
When one stoops to deceive!
The young handsome Lord,
Went mad with guilt and grief.

The cables of his mind,
Slowly unwound.
When his mistress's, body,
Was laid in the ground.

And there he would wander-
On the heights-by the coast.
For he was accompanied,
By a beautiful ghost.

And never-to the end of his life,
Was that Lord-though broken hearted,
With his spectral companion,
Ever parted.

That spirit-call it what you will!
Was his salvation.
For it whispered words of pardon,
And of consolation.

Her soul-she said-
With his-when he died-
Would roam the sea-both-
And merge with the tide.

Which-shows a noble spirit,
Though, with much life to live,
And herself-judged too harshly,
Yet-can forgive.

And many-who have walked the beach,
Often have told.
Of an image of a young girl-
Beautiful and bold.

That about the cliffs-
The castle ramparts,
The foaming, waves does trek-
And many a passing boat,
And many a ship wreck-
And many a drowning sailor,
Does she assist-
In ghostly garbs.

So the legend goes.

In the village,
The harbour,
And down by the bay,
The village people
Shake their heads
And then they say:

The rich handsome Lord,
Received two parcels,
The rich mad Lord,
Who lived in the castle,
The rich young Lord
Walked the cliffs eternally-
And lived with his mistress,
In the castle by the sea.

Nicholas Alexander Papantoniou

October 11 1987

THE ADVICE OF THE WHITE BIRD

Once, a beautiful white bird,
Flew down to me and said:
'I have flown so far-that my soul has bled.
A hundred more miles-and I would be dead.
I did not come all this way, for your bread,
But to give some advice-to your noble head.
To a mind, where sense has fled,
Hear my words and let them spread!'

'Forever is forever.
And never is never.
Are you really-Paul-so clever?
If you would think to sever,
Your life's greatest endeavour.
Your fears, your doubts, are only a tether,
Holding back your love-
For the beautiful Heather.
You must make-your choice-today!'

The bird told me so and off he flew.
Up through the clouds and into the blue!
But the meaning of his words-it grew and grew,
As I thought of me and I thought of you!
If that bird was real-then it might be true!
And what was I now-to do-to do?
To make a choice-I would not rue?

The past is past-I do not care,
Whether it was sad-or whether it was fair!
We have a lot of love to share.
We can love each other-if we dare!
Though our lives are long-no moment can we spare,
I think about your eyes, your hair-
If I lost you-then-my soul would tear!

So let us go-to where it's high!
Where the air is clear and words don't lie.
And we can touch the stars-if we try!
Where love is pure-without a sigh-
And freedom and truth never die!
The light of wonder is in the eye!
I love you and there is no why.

And what must be, must be, must be.
And what must be-then must be free!
The golden glory-I can see,
Will fill our hearts-both you and me,
With timeless joy, so utterly-
My life is good-if shared with she!
I pledge my troth-beloved-to thee-

Forever is forever,
And never is never,
Am I-Paul-really so clever?
If I would think to sever,
My life's greatest, endeavour,
My fears, my doubts, are only a tether,
Holding back my love-
For my beautiful Heather-
I will offer her my hand, today!

And thus in things of altitude,
I found my meaning offered,
In glory-coloured spectrums,
And flights-my dreams are covered!

Oh, soaring bird from somewhere strange,
Who flew so very far-to make me whole-
Thank you, for revealing-
The eternal freedom-of my soul!

SEPTEMBER 20   2009 7.08-8.59 a.m.

THE SUITOR
Or YIAGOTHOTIMIULAR   (1937. New York.)

I have often not wanted to marry-
From love and from duty.
I was told-while young-to marry-
An hereditary beauty!
The bigoted, blighted, baneful bones,
Of all my rich ancestors,
Breathed; 'money must marry money,'
It will open many doors!'

I acquiesced! Indeed I did!
I am a decadent young materialist.
I must look for the 'Eternal Feminine'-thought I-
I must seek that timeless tryst.

A Manhattan dwelling, doleful, dunce-I am.
With many wealthy uncles, aunts and friends!
A weary wastrel! Vapid, shallow-
An elegant, lazy bum-
A loafer-a free-loader-a flapper-a slacker!
Running up a tab-that never ends!

Not Dillinger,
Not Bonnie and Clyde,
Were ever more chastised for-
Nor chastened by-their sins and mistakes!
And where could I hide?
J. Edger Hoover and his G-men,
Couldn't have harried me more!
F.D.R. himself-couldn't have put me more to shame-
I was bruised and sore.
I took the blame.

A worthless hedonist-they call me-
Cruelly, they do!
A mellifluous, pleasure-seeking dope.
A languorous, ludicrous, superficial stiff,
At the end of a long financial rope!
I needed a rich wife, they said-you bet-
I was out of everything-but hope!

That was just swell.
I could not cry, 'Ixnay!' or even, 'Yowser!'

But would any dame-have the moxie?
Or would she take a powder-and go on the lam?
Would it be yea or nay-hunky-dory or nix-?
Would true love blossom-or go on the fritz?
I must surge and purge the urge-
To stay single-and merge-at once-
On the verge-I was-of wedded bliss or blight-
I needed a tomato-with lots of dough!
I pondered this-one morning-over
Coffee, orange juice, toast, eggs and ham-
Oh, the sad and spoilt and futile man that I am!

Was I finally going to do it?
Was I going to matrimonial Heaven?
That was the great question-for me-
In New York-that lovely,
Autumn-of 1937.

Was I simply-another sap?
Who didn't have the ap-
Titude-for high romance?
If I could only flap-my angel wings,
And tap-my way to-higher things!
I was in the lap-of the Gods.
Were all my dreams-only sigh dreams?
Or were they-do or die-dreams?
Or was it all just pap?
The thought makes me wince.
Would I have to take the rap-
For my sorry sins?
I never know what's best for me,
For I don't have a map-
To my true destiny.

Oh! A shallow man, a fallow man-
No roots in me do deep endure.
No constancy, no faith,
No fidelity will yield allure!

A feckless, spendthrift,
Creature of the jazz age-the roaring twenties-
Surfing along-through prohibition-
A misspent youth.
Dancing the Charleston,
Quaffing bootleg booze,
Worshiping Dempsey-
And deifying Ruth.

Ex-Yale, where I just exhaled-
But not excelled.
I learned little and drank a lot.
Not as able as I ought to be,
Not as strong as Charles Atlas.
Now I must grapple like
Jim Londos, with my dark fate.
Or swim like Johnny Weissmuller,
In deadly and uncharted, waters.

Love of sports, booze and, frails,
Brought me no rewards-
But only-not-so-innocent pleasure.
Now I must try to find-
A constantly yielding treasure!

I'm an optimist-yes-but also dumb-
And I think there is no certain cure.
Foolish am I-I am Foolish.
But my imbecility is pure!

Oh! In union-I say-holy or unholy!
The effervescence of my frothy life!
The fizz of it, the sparkle, the giddiness,
The dizziness, the strife!
The buzz, the bubbles, balloons-
All must end!
For I must-I shall-have a wife!

So, I looked around for a beauty.
I stooped me-to search around.
I inspected anything pretty in a dress,
In each passing burg or town.

And then!
After weeks
And weeks and weeks of looking,
I was very weak from looking-
One evening-in early October-
A day before the world series started-
(I was rooting for the Yankees-
And had put a bundle on them to win)-
Then-just after sunset-almost twilight.
On a quiet, balmy, tree lined
Street in Brooklyn-
I saw a raving beauty-
Just crossing the street.

The street was fairly deserted,
A few kids playing.
A few people walking.

I walked towards her.
She looked suddenly up at me.
Her grey eyes,
Did sparkle like diamonds.
Her thick, glossy black hair
Did shine like a moonlit night,
Her skin as was as pale as melting
Vanilla ice cream, on a hot summer day.
As slender as a stem-she was-
An ethereal quality-indeed she had.
A strange, soft, core or perhaps ore,
Of pure, super-concentrated,
Undiluted femininity!
She smiled slightly.
Her huge eyes warmed
With a profound hesitation,
And I fell in love-headlong falling-
Just then and there. I was gone.
It took one, two, three seconds. No more.
I never had before-nor ever did again.
Nothing rude, no turpitude-in her-could I find.
No discord to the syncopation of my heartbeat.
She did exude the purest light!
I could expiate for hours,
On her feminine virtues,
Corporeal and subliminal-
That assailed my being.
For she pulsated a delicate, radiance to me-
And believing is seeing.

Nothing vitiated the glory,
Of her fair fame, figure and face.
I could adduce no barrier-to my heart.
A romantic, I have never, ever been,
But they say-it is never too late-to start.
On bended knee, with bended will,
And bended reason-I offered her my all.
Impulsively, impetuously,
Irrationally, irresponsibly, irreparably.
A great schism, appearing-
Fracturing walls-twixt calculating brain cells-
And the mysterious ways of the heart.

I got down on one knee.
I spread my arms.
"Prithee," Said I,
"Beautiful lady, marry me today!
Pardon my suddenness!
And my being so fresh!
Before we've even been regularly introduced-
But I am desperate to make you mine!
Your aesthetic treasures,
Your bounty of beauty is mad,
In monstrous, profusion!
Have you any cash?
I care not! Not at all, not a whit!
I will suffer a contusion!
If you tell me 'nay',
Tell me 'yea.'
Here are you-here am I.
Don't sigh. Let us, only try.
Where are you from, my beauty?
Tell me now. Where do you go?
Whom-are your parents?
Your very relatives?
Instantly now, give me an answer!
Yea or nay?
My heart beats like an accelerated
Falcon in its furious, flowing, forward flight-
Fleeing from the fiercest of forest fires!

She looked at me-
With alternating hope and fear.
Hope won, and she spoke.
I rose to my feet,
In dizzy, expectation.
I was all attentive solicitude.

She spoke softly;
"Yiagothotimiular, is where I am from-
Yiagothotimiular, is where I must return to.
Yiagothotimiular, is where my parents dwell on,
Yiagothotimiular, is many light years and firmaments-
Far away, among-the distant, distant stars!
Yiagothotimiular, is beautiful beyond all words!"

So she said.
And her voice was so wonderful.
A full, soft, rich music-tender as silk-
Yet full of a mysterious, unfathomable power.

Then she smiled at me sadly and kindly.
She disappeared. Slowly-
It took a little more than three minutes-
She faded, gradually, her figure and face,
Inexorably waxed and wavered and waned
And washed away-away-so very slowly.
But her voice rang on, clearly and true-
Like a great chiming bell in a storm,
To the very last.

"Now, beloved,
I can return to my own, Yiagothotimiular.
To my homeland-to my parent's planet-
Beyond-the furthest star.
Farewell, my love-you have just set me free!
I have waited for ages-
Oh, how long, can ages be!
I have waited for a mortal man-
To love me once-forever-and at first sight.
I have waited for-a single man-
To show that human, loving light!
It breaks the spell of Akantrazo-
Who cast me here on earth-
In revenge for the death of Discartopha ,
Back on my ancient, alien hearth.
Until the love of mortal male-
Could liberate the chains-
The chains of time and space-
Oh, how weary are the chains!
I speak of love-of love-not bestial-but celestial,
Though, indeed-ah, indeed-I am an extraterrestrial!
And it is love I feel-pure love-earthling-for you.
I journey home at last-with joy!
But in that single, dazzling, glowing moment-
I have known and felt and touched and thought-
The love of mortal man and mortal woman-
Here on earth, for full, rich, long and loving lives.
I have therefore paid in full-the cosmic tithes-
Oh, how long and how loving, are such lives!
I will love you forever and ever,
Though we will never meet again!
My journey-an instant for me-never to return-
Across aeons and stardust and galaxies-
So awesome and glorious and wondrous and far-
For I now return with great, great joy-
To my beloved-Yiagothotimiular!"

She spread her pale, slender hands,
Now almost transparent-reaching-in my direction.

"For just a few more moments-
In this dimension-here am I-here you are.
Soon, I leave this curious land of skyscrapers, children,
Of crowds, parks, bus and car.
To a place-where-between beauty and wonder,
Truth and glory-there is no bar-
For I go back now-toYiagothotimiular!"

"Soon I will see once again-a beautiful sunset-
On the hills, of Avshantaar!
And roam and dwell on the diamond shores,
And floating flowers, of Kunipar!
Take heed, O my beloved mortal-
For soon-is coming a great war.
Yet now after long, long exile,
I return to Yiagothotmiular!"

She-for I never knew her name-had nearly faded,
She was now, all but invisible, a faint trace.
I could just about perceive her pale, blue outline.
Her face, her smile, her eyes,
Were full of an unearthly tenderness
And serenity and all-encompassing love
And kindness and sweetness-
As she gazed at me,
And she spoke,
For the last time.

"Farewell, treasured mortal-I do not know your name!
Do not forget me-I will not forget you-fear you not!
I must go now-my own darling-on a journey, interstellar,
For as you see-my beloved-I am not an earth dweller!
My heart will be with you always-
Your heart will be with me.
Love lasts as long as love can wish-
It lasts eternally!
Though but for one blessed,
Shining moment-that we shared-
That nothing can ever mar!
For now time and space cannot dent me,
Do not in the future-ever repent me.
Remember that the love-you sent me,
Sent me back-
To Yiagothotimiular!"

So she said,
The last word was in a great, long,
Lingering echo, lasting for several seconds
And she was blowing me a kiss,
Through the pale, blue,
Billowing, clouds of vapour,
That had surrounded and
Enveloped her since
She first began to speak,
From a portal-if such indeed it was-
In time and space!

I had watched and listened, too stunned,
Too shocked, too amazed-too bowled over-
To speak or reason well.
I was in a daze.
I cried, "Goodbye."
I reached out my hand for her.
But-she was already gone.
All that remained of her now-
Was a drifting, swirling, cobalt haze-
Where her pale, delicate, beauty once stood!

Just discovered, just left.
Just found, just gone.
Just loved, just lost.
Just won. Just went.
Just like that.
I sighed, I shook my head,
I stamped my foot!
Darn!

I turned and began walking.
It was dark now, and cool,
And I had to catch a bus for Manhattan.

Perhaps-I thought-true love-
All true love-is lost-if a man only once-blinks.
In an instant-vanished.
That is the way-an iceberg-an ocean liner sinks.
And sometimes-a man so thirsty for true love-
Loses the cup-ere he drinks-
Like me! Was it real bad, first-time luck?
Was it a jinx? I know not!
Perhaps a man is never as sure of love-
As he thinks-when he is young

And joyous and carefree.

Oh well!
I had-tomorrow-a baseball game to go to.
It was a bother-it was a pain-
It was a blow-it was a shock-
It was a jolt-it was a boor-it was a jar.
For my one and only-ever true love-
Had just gone back-
To yiagothotimiular.

March 1 2011 2.37-2.41.a.m.

CHALLENGE

The challenge for the thinker,
And perhaps-you can find it out-
Is how-
To ask, to question,
To wonder,
And not to doubt.

The challenge for the warrior,
And perhaps-you can read his fate-
Is how-
To fight, to battle,
To conquer,
And not to hate.

Nicholas Alexander Papantoniou

Nov 15   2009   2.50.-4.55.a.m.

THE GHOST ON THE PATIO

I drove one night on business,
South to sweet old Dixie land,
Through the sprawling bible-belt,
On my way to Dallas, Texas.
To a red-neck, blue-collar, apple-pie,
Old-fashioned, hick- town,
And stopped there for the night. Dog-tired.
Had me a good meal-and plenty of it too,
Good, old southern, traditional, belt-busting,
Wholesome, all-American food.
The kind of food that made the good ol' U.S.of A.
Into the undisputed and indisputable,
No 1 world champ, super-power.

The landlord of the establishment-
An old motel-just off the highway-
Was a tall, big, lumbering, powerful, fat,
Pink-faced, cheerful, obliging man.
Mr. Harry Dieter Burghoff.
6'5, 325, German-American,
Blue-eyed, bass-voiced, bull-necked, crew-cut.
Just as normal and natural as could be.
We got to talking, as strangers do sometimes.
Politics. Sport. Current topics. Says he:

"I don't get me too many visitors
Staying over, you know,
Just for the chow, you're tired and
I'll show you to your room.
But I'm an honest man,
So I'll tell you straight.
If, when you're in bed, you hear
A muffled voice, calling you outside,
Do not go-I tell you-do not go!
You'll see the ghost on the patio!"

I asked Mr. Burghoff,
To tell me about it.

"Well, he walks and moans,
And breaths and reels around,
(Like this) and that (He showed)
Kinda to and fro.

If you see him, hear him or feel him,
He can tell-right off the bat-
You're new and green and so-
He has no equal, in these parts-
Not high or low.
It's the ghost on the patio!"

"It's not for kicks, nor for show,
Nor laughs-does he do it-
Not for comedy.
But decades of weary, wandering woe!
Back in them days-crime was quick-
And the law was slow.
And because of this,
There's a ghost on my patio!"

"They cornered him and robbed him,
And beat him and murdered him-
Then and there-that night-
While he screamed, 'No, no, no!'
Some seen them run and run away.
Now, I have the most haunted patio."

"His poor head was crushed to bits,
With each terrible, crunching blow!
By ruthless burglars,
And robbers and muggers,
Who criminally ebb and flow,
And killed the man-just outside my place-
Whose soul now struts upon my patio!"

"A sweet, kind, meek, mild, skinny little man,
With (they say) the eyes of a doe.
And he was-most instantly-turned into,
The ghost on my own patio."

"I wished they had caught and hung those
Cowardly, rat-fink, murdering bastards-
Or fried them on old sparky-
Yes Sir! Oh, I do. Oh!
For they produced-the miscreants-
The wretched, danged ghost upon my patio."

"He comes and goes,
From midnight, to one or two or three.
Just each and every blamed night,
'Tween the moon and the sun-

You don't tell me! I know!
The guy who prances-
The ghost who dances!
And kinda likes his chances,
On my godam patio!"

"The first night he ever showed up,
On the patio-outside-over by that there tree-
I thought, 'Whoa!
'Was that a ghost just I see-
Out there-a gesturing at me?'
I made the sign of the cross,
I was truly at a loss-
But I'm the boss-of this place.
I was alone,
Late, that cold, howling, wild, windy night-
And I sure don't easy take fright-but-
I had to know-because-darn it -I just had to!
If there really was-a spirit out there-
A dwelling out on a patio!
I went out to see-and sure enough-
There he was-a wobbling around."

"So, that very first night I seen him-
Years ago-I went to bed and
I was up and down all night,
Just like a regular, blamed yo-yo.
For I so feared I would see,
That darned ghost again-
Smirking-at me-real eerily,
Just a few yards away from the bed-
The drat wraith of the patio."

Mr.Burghoff, leaned forward, confidingly,
And lowered his deep voice-a little-
So the other diners-about a dozen or so-
Some of who had small children,
Would not overhear him.
Hulking shoulders, hunching,
With a certain repressed excitement,
And after easing the creases of his bull-like neck,
He went on;

"Well, you see-
He moves with no noise!
With elegance and poise-
Seems like-he just toys-

With the whole darn place!
He works his way around-by and by-
Moving real smooth and easy,
Like a knife-through a pie.
Just goes right through-it all-that's no lie-
Through walls, ceilings and floors.
He sure don't need no windows.
He sure don't need no doors.
I reckon, he is attracted by all
The racket and snores of the sweetly
And peacefully sleeping!"

"Now whether we have a sweltering heat wave,
Or whether we have several inches of snow,
Or whether we have twisters on the go,
I still got me an infernal-ghost on my new patio."

"It's as regular as clockwork,
I think this ghost's a real pro-
And I'll always have me a spirit-
Floating around, making mischief, cutting capers,
Out on my patio."

"Heck, I had me customers-running out-
Buck, bare-assed, naked, some of 'em-
Male and female-
Four or five nights, in a row!
Screaming, jumping, hollering,
A-shaking-a-trembling-a-quivering-a bouncing-
A whirling around!
Eyes a-popping out of their heads-
Some even busting out-into tears,
Jabbering on like confounded lunatics-
Because I had me a ghost-
Sojourning-there on that patio!

Well, that's not real good for business!
Word gets around pretty quick.
I lost so many regulars-
Wouldn't even drop by to say 'hello.'
See, most folk don't want no spookiness at all-
At nights-no sir-they just like things
Real pleasant, easy and mellow.

My beautiful girlfriend-Debbie-my one true love-
Who I wanted to marry real bad-took off-
Told me she couldn't live in such

A terrible, creepy haunted place-
It was either the haunted place-or her.

So she left.
Customers left.
My staff mostly left.
Said-they didn't sign up for no ghosts-
In no kitchens-no way. I stayed.
But gracious sakes! I felt most abandoned!
But the good Lord gave me comfort and courage.
Soon, I got pretty used to it and wasn't bothered, too much, no more!
Now, I always had a few guns around-naturally.
'Course-only for self-defence-
But guns ain't no dern good against-
A spectral intruder like this-
Against a body that don't have a body.

Had me a whole heap of trouble.
I had me one regular
Customer named, Joe!
Now, he was such a drunk-
He weren't hardly ever sober-
Didn't make no difference to him-
Ghosts or no ghosts-he mostly lived in a
Alcohol induced stupor-anyways-
You may say. I told him plain and blunt;
'Joe! Don't know, if you know this-There's a ghost,
Goes around the place. Comes out, nights!'
He said:"Really? A ghost? Oh, now that's real nice!
Real nice! That's just perfectly delectable! Ho, ho, ho!
Hey, now-I'll drink-to that rowdy, darned, deadbeat
Ghost-out there on your patio!"

I racked my brains out to figure,
What I done in my life-to deserve such a blamed,
Lousy throw-of the dice!
I busted a few heads, in fights-
I guess-when I was younger-
But they were fights, which,
Sure as heck-I didn't-no way-start!
I busted a few bones-playing football-as a linebacker-
But I just done what the coach told me-
And what anybody else on the team
Would have done in my place-just as quick.
But, I reckon, there ain't no
Real way of calculating, these things,
For human beings.

Anyways, things were all haywire,
And crazy and just about unbelievable-
All on account, of that darn,
Unnatural, wispy, little ghost on my patio!"

"He's out there-always-a-waiting-
A-watching-a creeping-a jiggling-
A floating, a flipping, a flopping, or a flapping!
A-looking, a-noticing-all night you see-
Looking for strange, different, new folks
To introduce himself to.
Just like a godam, pestilential
Vulture or albatross, or scavenger-or crow!
Once I was almost-driven to drink-
Just like Joe-right to the very brink-
And once-I thought I saw-the ghost-wink-at me-
But now I'm philosophical,
About, the ghost on the patio."

"I ain't no blamed coward neither!"
Harry Dieter Burghoff, protested,
His sky-blue eyes bulging and widening,
Running a massive, powerful hand
Through his short, orange hair,
Now damp with sweat.
"No sir! I come from real tough,
Old German stock, on both sides of the family!
Prussians! And some of my military ancestors-
Died decorated! Fighting in many wars!
Oh, as far back as Frederick the great.
I had me one relative-
Oh-about seventy-five years ago-
That was a famous, circus strongman,
Well documented fact. Toured
The world too-between the wars!
But getting back to the main point.
I ain't superstitious either!
And if I was scared-well, let me tell you-for a fact-
I would have left long, long, ago-with my Debbie!
You see, to me, it's just a matter of principle.
Back in the old days-them frontier settlers-didn't get
Chased off their spreads by no Indians-nor hardships-
Hot summers-cold winters-twisters-nor Mexicans-
You always got to remember the Alamo!
I got nothing against Mexicans-mind-
I know plenty of Mexicans-
They're real nice, friendly, regular,

Neighbourly, peacable people!
Still, don't get me started on the subject of illegal immigration!
The government has just about give up on it!
It's a real contentious issue around here anyway!
But what I mean to say is-I ain't about to be
Chased off my own, rightful place and property by-
No wandering, unhinged, blamed ghost-dancing around.
Oh, it wouldn't be right!
But-see- this spooky thing-
It seems to spread and wallow and grow,
So, I guess, I'll never, ever get rid of
This ghost on my patio."

Mr.Burghoff, sighed
And shook his head, sadly.

"I say's to him once-for I cornered him once-
I say's to him-looking at him boldly, straight in the eye,
One dark winter night-I say's to him:

"Listen here now, Mr.Ghostman!
Now, I'm a fair man and I'm a patient man,
But there are limits! We got to settle this now!
Don't you have nowhere else, to go to?
Ain't there, no one else,
You can give a scary show to?
Don't you reckon some other residences,
Might appreciate you visiting them?
You're ruining my family business-
Can't you give some other folks,
A spooky throw-too?"

But he just sort of shrugs at me,
And smiles and then his shape,
Just started to get sorta, melty, quivery and fluttery
And began to disappear,
Bend, blend and split and flow,
Seven different ways.
And I knew then and there-
Deep in my heart-
I would never, ever get shot or rid of
The ghost on my patio."

So said, Mr.Burghoff
Candidly and somberly.

I told him-as kindly and politely as I could-

For I was growing very tired-
I did not care a rap for this superstition,
I did not give a little toe-tap,
For this vain, old-fashioned, southern tradition,
And-privately-I really wondered-
At his mental condition.

"Really, Mr. Burghoff!
I'm much obliged for the very delicious meal,
And I'm genuinely sorry about how you feel,
But this-just isn't real.

This is-you know, the 21st century,
Go see a psychiatrist-or a doctor-
Or a therapist-first visit on me!"
I said goodnight, thanked him kindly again-
Most sincerely-
And in my room-undressing-
I burst out and laughed aloud-
At the ghost of his patio.

At twelve o'clock I went to bed.
I slept soundly-or I thought I did-
And suddenly awoke.
And looked around in the dark-
And afterwards the memory,
Of it was a terrifying tableau.

For I wondered if the small, pale, lone figure-
Standing-calmly-waiting-
In the middle of the room-
A blurry, translucent blue and green, grey and white-
Was the ghost of the patio?

At two o'clock I dressed, packed, paid.
Said a quick goodbye, had to fly, my oh my!
And I was Dallas, Texas bound,
Once more and glad of it,
And-as they say here-I won't be back 'no mo',
For I had seen the ghost-the terrible ghost-
The ghost on the patio.

Harry D.Burghoff smiled,
And waved, good naturedly, jovially,
Nodded-knowingly.
And then shook his head-to himself-
Softly and sardonically.

For him it was a normal routine.
He had seen his share-I declare.
As I drove away I saw
Harry Burghoff's, huge frame,
Shrinking, in my rear view mirror,
Clearly silhouetted, in the neon lights
As he stood-bearlike-
Outside his motel.

Yes, oh yes indeed!
He knew why I had to go.
For I had looked into the pale, blank,
Vacant eyes of the ghost.
And I had heard the faint, vapid,
Muffled voice of the ghost.
And I had felt the light, soft,
Cold touch of the ghost.
As I had sat in the dark, on my bed-
A little after one fifteen .a.m.

I had-at first-looked around me,
Blinking-in the darkness.
Until, I heard a slight, strange noise.
I felt something smooth touch
My shoulder-like an icy feather-and lo-
I looked up and I saw-

The horrible ghost,
The terrible ghost,
The awful ghost,
The hideous, dreadful,
Supernatural, faintly glowing,
Billowing-undulating-wavering-slanting-folding-
And very softly sighing ghost.

And the ghost who had turned to me,
And smiled and nodded slowly,
And then pointed a steady,
Transparent finger right-directly-at me,
And faintly-oh so very softly and faintly-
Whispered out-my full name.
And then said:
"Welcome."

And you see,
It was-
The ghost on the patio.

NOVEMBER 27-29   1994

DANCING BELINDA
OR A SONG OF AUSTRAILIA

I remember my love-
A love that failed.
Through the mists of time.
T'was many years ago,
I heard his voice
And his request,
Which I refused.

I met him in Sydney
He had come from Darwin.
And had lived in Melbourne
Adelaide and Alice springs.
He had worked in Brisbane
And in Perth.
He wished to settle
On Queensland earth.
At an age when girls
Are fond of romancing-
And I was just nineteen
And fancied dancing.

He was twenty four,
Too 'old' for me.
But, I could not help
Watching him on and off-all that night,
Through the bouncing crowds of the party,
Listening, to the roaring, big band, swing music.
And he watched me too-blushing-
Sly and shyly-I noticed-
Like a guilty, shamefaced little schoolboy.

I thought of him that night,
Looking up at the starry sky,
When in my cosy, warm bed.
Not dwelling on my usual,
Happy, mellow, bedtime thoughts-
I thought of him instead.
Kissing my clean, white pillow-
As though it were his head.

He was handsome,
Tall, very slim but muscular.
Pale blue eyes,
Dark brown hair.
And a face-and body
Bronzed, by the sun.
Both rugged and boyish-
Of masculine beauty.

I was then-tall, fit and slender.
Considered very good looking.
Very blonde, blue eyed, very freckled.
Athletic-from a lot of swimming and tennis,
Both of which-I excelled at.
I was of a 'good' family,
Which is to say 'well off.'
And very 'proper'.
I was a bit of a loner.
A little bit introverted.

My parents were lovely.
My morals-from an upbringing-
In a strict Christian household,
My father a local preacher,
My mother a history teacher,
Were 'high'-but very honest.

My parents did not like him.
They much preferred the bank clerk
Who had been courting me, all that winter.
Though he was gawky, tall and thin,
Buck-toothed, red-haired
And had a piping, alto voice.
He was of 'good family',
And had 'high' prospects at the bank.
Though he was spineless, boring and a 'yes' man.
His hobby was collecting butterflies.
I wished to see those
Lovely creatures free-
Not pinned in a book.
I knew if I married him, I too
Might be pinned in a tidy book
And put on a dust-free shelf.

Neither mother nor father
Liked my new suitor.
He had no prospects,

No trade-except as a sort of
Itinerant mechanic-
And of his family-
The Lord alone knew.

But I knew his qualities
Far better than they.
He was not 'polite', or 'urbane'
He was a rough diamond,
And rather profane.

Yes, he was rough but honest.
And tough but gentle
After a few jars too many
He was quite sentimental-
But that was rare.
He asked me out.

Mother said, 'no'
Father said, 'no'
I said, 'no', once-
And then I said, 'yes.'

He was frank and forthright.
He had few pretensions-and little fear.
He mostly lived-for fun, cars, sports and beer.
He had thick, dark eyebrows, a hairy chest.
His boyish yet manly features, blazed his
Every thought. He knew nothing at all
Of dissimulation, nor hiding his views,
But more honest he was than thousands,
Who mask their thoughts and words,
In cloaks of artifice and a mirage of diplomacy.
A blunt, brave fellow, he was,
As free as the birds,
That fly over our vast country,
Sparsely populated,
But rich and dense
In love and freedom.

He was rather critical of
Our lovely and very dear English cousins-or-
'Those ruddy pommy poofters',
As he called them.
He had never, ever forgotten
Nor forgiven them for the infamy of
'Bodyline' bowling.

But he was very far from being
Alone in that prejudice-among
Australians, at that time.
His great hero was
The immortal, Don Bradman,
Whom he worshiped,
And had seen play many times.
When he spoke of him-his eyes-
Would light up like a child.

He said once-that
I had the figure and face of a Goddess.
He said once that my hair was the colour
Of pure sunshine.
He said that my eyes were the colour
Of the summer sky.
He said I had the smile of an angel.
And he said my freckles-were beautiful.

I'll never forget his voice-
Deep, gruff and flat.
I remember his 'G'day!'
And 'morning Belinda!'
'See yer tomorrow Belinda!',
And 'fancy a spin Belinda?'
Before, we went for a drive.
He drove extremely fast-but very well.

And more eloquent-
His tone of voice was
Than volumes of atrophied prose,
Semantic artifice-
Tactful constipation,
Or academic diarrhoea lying,
On my father's, dusty, creaking shelves.

That first night and others-
We went dancing together.
We would go out four-
Five nights a week.
Sometimes we met
In the afternoons as well,
At the beach. Swam. Picnics.
Went to the fun-fairs.
Ate lots of ice-cream.
It was such a long, lovely, beautiful,
Australian summer.

So we danced together-
All of the summer-oblivious-
While huge, dark,
Ominous, storm clouds
Were slowly gathering, rolling-
Converging-all across the world.

We were dancing and talking
And laughing and we ate and
Went to movies-
Walked-holding hands-
Till about eleven.
Then he would drive me home.
He was my first ever boyfriend-he knew that.
So-I think-he was on his 'best' behaviour.
I think he saw me-and my family-as 'posh',
But we weren't.
He was always a gentleman,
According to his moral lights-
Always, with me anyway.
He said once earnestly,
That he had a 'bucket load',
Of respect for me.

One night we quarrelled.
Over a girl he had once known,
And we bumped into-while on the
Way to a dancing club.
An 'old flame'.
A, 'fast', or, 'easy', or, 'fun' girl,
A ,'goer', 'understanding'-
Meaning-compliant.
Surprised-caught off guard,
I was angry-I was quite quick tempered
Back then-and after the girl had gone-
I told him a few things-with no mincing of words.
It was the only quarrel we ever had.
The only cross words we ever spoke.

I'll never forget his deep, sad voice
As he took my hand in his-
Large and strong-and begged
For my forgiveness.
He said:

"Entrancing, Belinda,
O ' dancing, Belinda,
O 'dancing, Belinda!
Will you come, dancing,
Belinda, tonight?"

I said:
"No sir, I won't,
I will not sir, I won't."

He sighed deeply and loosed
His hold on my hand reluctantly-
And turned and left.
I never saw him again.

For the world was changing.
The war came.
Europe was in turmoil.
The Germans, for the second time
In a little over twenty years
Threatened to overrun, Western Europe.
And this time they succeeded.

The valiant, disciplined, fanatical troops
Of Adolf Hitler's, third Reich,
Soon covered that continent-
From Norway in the north-
To Greece in the south.
From France in the west-
To Poland in the east.
And then, they turned on Russia.

But the war also carried on
In the far east-after Japan's
Surprise attack on Pearl harbour.
And in the northern part of Africa,
Where the British and her Empire,
Did all to hold its ground,
As Rommel-arriving to help the Italians-
Swept them straight back Into Libya and Egypt,
And seemed poised
To take, the Suez Canal,
And cut the British off-from the empire-
Their life-line.

My rough diamond, volunteered
At the first day's, opportunity.
My bank clerk, stayed at home
Throughout the war,
Feigning chronic asthma,
And flat feet.

So I stayed at 'home'.
At once, I volunteered as a nurse.
While my true love-went off-
To the exotic land of camels,
Palm trees and pyramids,
Of Bedouins and Arabs and scorching,
Blazing, burning desert sands-went off-
To fight the mighty Afrika Korps-
Led by the redoubtable Rommel.

At least,
I did not marry
The bank clerk,
I sent him off with scorn.
When I had time,
I haunted the floors of the
Dancing clubs,
Where-my one true love-
Was born-
And I wept.

Months past.
War came to Australia,
Through our brave troops,
Who answered the call to battle,
As their parents had before-
In the Great War.

Now-as a nurse I had
All too many opportunities
To see the terrible, suffering that war
Brought to soldiers,
And to their loved ones.
I did my job
With grim efficiency.

The great German eastward, blitzkrieg-
Had stalled in Russia, as winter fell.

Singapore fell disastrously, to the Japanese.
The fortress of Tobruk-
At first-garrisoned by Australians-
Under Moreshead-
Finally fell, to the bold, daring Rommel.
And then I had but little news-
And mostly bad.

I listened hopefully to
Winston Churchill's, speeches.
Read all the papers.
Tried not to think of the danger.
But every time I heard
'Lili Marlene,' playing -
Or some of 'our' love songs,
Or dancing numbers-
I remembered and thought of him-
And prayed that he was safe.

During the first battle of El Alamein,
The intrepid Rommel, attacked furiously,
Sensing-total victory in North Africa.
But he lacked the numbers,
And resources to break through.
Then-after a pause of months-there came a great battle
Called the 2nd battle of El Alamein-
Near Alexandria-the British 8th army,
Slowly and carefully built up by
The cautious Montgomery-now-
Greatly superior-in numbers, of tanks and men-
And with air supremacy, finally
Defeated the German panzers.
Rommel-massively outnumbered-
By the British-in both men and tanks-
With hugely extended and precarious supply lines,
Starved of fuel-which went as a priority to Russia-
Or was sunk, by the British navy, before it reached him-
And without air support-desperately,
Flung his tough, truculent veterans-
Towards Alexandria-
And was turned back.

This battle and-even more-
The German disaster at Stalingrad,
A little over two months ahead-
Turned the tide of the whole war.

A month later,
Came a letter for his family.
Soon-I too heard the news.

He had fallen bravely,
In a moonlit attack.
On October 23rd 1942.

Home on leave,
Some army friends of his-
Sought me out-at his request.
They said that he was,
'Always talking about me'-
And had called me,
His 'angel Belinda'.

They told me of his death.
He had fallen-
With several others-
Cut down, by German guns.

My true love,
Had died bravely,
Running to the front line,
During, the infantry attack.
Calling;

"Let's get 'em boys!
Can't let the pom's, have the best of it!
Move yer asses! Straight ahead!
Australia, forever!"
Then he was shot.

He did not die at once,
They told me-
But lay for a while smiling,
Grimacing and groaning.
His last words were:
"Tell Belinda, tell Belinda,
Tell Belinda-
I love her." He said.
And then,
He died.

And now the years
Have passed.
My hair is grey-

And white-in parts
And I am old.

For all these many years,
I have thought of him,
His words, his smile, his voice,
His laughter-his carelessness-
His innocence-haunted me.

For though I married,
And have children
And grandchildren-
And great grandchildren soon-
I did not marry, for true love,
But for honest affection, respect,
And esteem-and a love of children.

I married a good, decent,
Honest and honourable man,
Who loved me-I liked him very much-
And I have been very happy-in a way.
But I have dreamed, all these years
Of him-that died so long, long, ago.

If you should weep,
Who read this,
Then I too shed a tear,
For he had few pretentions
And little fear.
But much, much love,
And love for me,
And for his dog and his beer,
His sports, his cars and his fun,
And his fellows,
His country and his flag.

After he died,
I took his dog,
Walter, home with me.
He asked me once if
I would do so
And I said, 'yes.'
When Walter-
Who missed his master
As much as I did-died-
A few years later,
I buried him,

In my garden.

Now, sometimes-when I'm in bed-
The soft, clean, pillow beneath my gray old head-
I think of where my long life, has led,
I think of the words,
The last words to me,
He ever said:

"Entrancing, Belinda,
O' dancing, Belinda,
O 'dancing, Belinda!
Will you come, dancing
Belinda, tonight?"

I said:
"No sir, I won't,
I will not sir, I won't."

I wonder where
All the time went-
I wonder what it truly meant,
So much life and love unspent,
And I repent.
I bitterly repent.

And sometimes and oh, yes, yes, I know-
You'll just call me a silly, old fool.
But, late at night-
Gazing up at the stars-
I look forward to dancing
Once again with him-in heaven-
Where I know-I absolutely know-
That he is waiting for me.

I think of him, always.
A man who died
So our nations honour
Would not loose,
It makes me think of wallabies,
Dingoes, wombats,
And kangaroos.

It makes me think of
Our nation's, children and youth.
Of our young country,
A home of hope and truth-

That he so loved.

It makes me think
Of our young love's-failure,
And it makes me think of
Our land-
Australia.

November 19   2010   11.29-11.38.p.m

JENNY

Jenny is walking on the beautiful, seashore.
By sunset, by dawn, by moonlit beams.
This vision-of her-and of the triumph of the beautiful-
Always lights my dreams!

Where have you been to jenny?
Where have you come from?
Where are you going jenny?
And-Jenny-whom do you love the most?
I wish I knew.

But jenny could not answer me.
Jenny-so blonde, so slim, so cool, so 1970's-flower child.
She could not tell me-where she had been-
Or where she had come from-or where she was going,
She could not say-whom she loved the most.
And the reason she could not answer-was-
Jenny was a ghost.

July 19   2010   4.40-5.25.a.m

THE MESSAGE

The quotidian of life,
Not the madness of fever,
Formed my beautiful days,
And joy was the lever.

A contiguous diffinity,
A continuum of woe.
A dithyramb of angels,
And it had to go!

I understand it all-now,
In a perspective anthropologic,
I understand it all,
With retrospective logic.

The provenance of my words,
And my prehensile mind,
Will be proven in the future,
As you-noble reader-will find.

With measurements, statistics, facts,
And aggregates and figures.
The magic code that seals them,
Is the code that also triggers.

The perfidious technocrat-
Always frothing with didactic bubbles.
In ontological ways,
Will be reduced to rubble.

The corona of my life,
The addendum of my thoughts and powers,
You will see-O faithful reader-
In epistemological hours!

In anatreptic times,
Our antediluvian patterns,
Sometimes follow Jupiter or Neptune,
Sometimes Venus, Mars or Saturn.

A moribund mutiny,
Of seraphic devils.
Lamenting-too late-the rotting fruit,
Of all their evils.

A lambent music-indeed-
Accompanied my travels.
Like a lapidary lesson,
You remember-when it unravels.

A tenebrous tenor, sung in the distance,
A sibilant soprano-also sang in sorrow.
They sang, 'Woe is me, woe is me, woe is me,
Tomorrow, tomorrow, tomorrow!'

A parallax vision had I,
Of things-far off-this day,
And the closer that I came,
The further they went away.

No recondite recidivism,
Overcame the sights I saw.
But a weary, desperate persiflage,
That numbed me to the core.

With a chiaroscuro evening,
A sunset-twilight-pianissimo.
As the day was leaving,
Foretold-tomorrow-fortissimo.

An incipient arabesque,
From a fool of a terpsichorean,
Lost many of life's labours and hopes,
As you-O heroic reader-no doubt-will have seen.

This message is a message is a message,
To all-who see it.
But the message cannot be a message,
Until, you can free it.

The sublunary tergiversations,
Led to a paean of sin.
The entropy of virtue,
Must be reversed-to win.

The palpitations and fibrillations,
Shook the base of truth,
Yet the light shone forth-for all to see-
Both in age and in youth!

The valleys and the plains of this alien place-
Were beautiful in extreme.
But the mountains and seas and skies-
Were supreme!

Difficult things are not so difficult,
If they are try-able.
For a life without the things I speak of,
Would not be viable.

I leave it to you-O beautiful reader,
To do what you must do!
For if you do not do it-
Who is going to?

I place it with you-O wonderful reader-
To open the message, the puzzle, the code!
And the one who does it,
Will be on the diamond road.

I cast no animadversions,
On the one who shared my dinner,
I do not care to talk about it,
Until I am thinner.

So I leave you to your task,
Your mystery, your puzzle and your quest!
I say, goodnight, farewell, goodbye to you-
To you, and all the rest!

August 21   2010   1.2-1.4.a.m.

BEAM

I walked into light that was,
Lighter than any light,
I had ever seen!

It saw through me-
I was joyously transparent-
And it knew all
I would be-
Could be-
Should be-
Or had been.

My mind was filled with joy-
Wonder, truth-glory and beauty-
Like a cobalt embolism.
And so I grew and I grew,
And I grew and I grew-
And I grew-
In optimism.

Nicholas Alexander Papantoniou

September 5-9   2010

**THE QUEEN OF PARADISE
OR A LOST LEGEND FROM A TIME
BEFORE RECORDED HISTORY**

I will tell thee now-
A tale of an ancient time,
Beneath our eternal skies.
For once there was a great queen-
Who was known by all as-
The queen of paradise.

Now I crave the truth of life and love,
But I have no device,
That can unlock the great mystery-
Of the queen of paradise.

A warrior queen-like none ever seen-
In brutal, warlike enterprise.
So fled the men-who feared this foe-
The queen of paradise.

Whether in savage irony-or simple truth-
No knowledge quite supplies,
The source of her symbolic name or title-
'The Queen of Paradise.'

Her beauty was beauty beyond compare!
Though she never used it-to charm or entice.
So pure-was the heart and soul and spirit,
Of the queen of paradise!

Her eyes on heaven-her heart with God-
She wished to sever all earthly ties.
'I care not if I please man-if I only please God!'
Quoth, the queen of paradise.

Thus her deeds were later mocked,
Cursed, denied-but she will always rise.
For greatness was the birthright of-
Our queen of paradise.

As fierce as a falcon, or a soaring eagle-
In smiting the foe! No need to eulogize-
For all men knew this-who fought with her,
For her-or against her-
Sweet, queen of paradise.

And all who knew her, loved her most-
Who knew her best-I sympathize.
For never was a great woman-
So afterwards slandered,
As the queen of paradise.

With her own great sword-she cut down the enemy.
Her name alone would paralyze!
Her foes-parted-as night parts-for the rising sun-
When she led her army in person-that great heroine-
The queen of paradise.

I am old now, my time-please God-is short-
But still-I must tell and sing and rhapsodize-
Of the lost legends,
The forgotten conquests,
The hushed and hidden fables,
From a long vanished, glorious age-the age-
Of the queen of paradise!

Before the time of the magnificent Greeks,
The mighty Romans and the great Germanic tribes,
She was a peerless legend of beauty and bravery,
The timeless queen of paradise.

Though millennia and centuries have passed,
As time and legend swiftly flies.
Still stands the story-stands she still-
In all her naked glory,
O' Queen of paradise!

Her long hair was of gold-
Her voice-was like music-a soft contralto-
That soothed and stirred and warmed-her eyes-
Were cobalt blue, large, wide-set, steady-
Thou dove-like queen of paradise!

She was very tall and very strong-very straight-
Though slim, broad shouldered.
(Men lusted after her breasts,
Her buttocks and her thighs.)

For her womanly beauty was truly breathtaking,
Ah, queen of paradise!

And loud was her voice-when calling to her army,
Her beloved, white horse-Lunato-was of great size.
Her men would follow her to hell or to heaven-follow-
The swirling, blazing sword-
Of the queen of paradise!

Through oceans of blood she waded-for her people,
Though peace was not always her prize!
For she loved the ring of victory, conquest and of triumph!
The dark queen of paradise.

The tales, the legends,
The romances of her battles,
They need-indeed-no slight reprise.
For I too fought and flew-wingtip to wingtip-
When young-with the daring queen of paradise.

No Amazon, no Viking, no Teuton,
No Spartan woman was purer-nor stronger-
Nor more steadfast-nor so wise,
As the virgin queen-who's pale, lovely flesh-
No man, no woman-had ever fully seen!
The elusive queen of paradise!

But kind as a cooing dove.
Loving all children, all animals,
And who cannot empathize?
For this was a queen-a towering queen-
True, queen of paradise.

She gave up her life to save
A hundred hostage children,
To show how a great queen dies.
And none must ever forget that base treachery
Ended the golden reign of-
The queen of paradise.

Why such things happen-who can say?
Who can tell the how's and when's and why's?
Was it God-or fate-or man-who brought the fall of
The queen of paradise?

The men that curse her-and curse her most-
Even among these-no one denies,
The achievements, the victory's,
The long forgotten glories,
Of the unquenchable queen of paradise!

None shall forget her childlike glee,
Her songs, her laughter-
Or her joyous battle cries!
For all good and bad-light and dark-
Great and terrible-dwelt-
Within the bounteous bosom,
Of the eternal queen of paradise!

But she was just and kind and merciful-
As well-be it said.
She loved her worshiping soldiers-
For them it did suffice-
To serve and fight and die for the ruler
Of their hearts, minds and souls-
Thou most wonderful queen of paradise!

She was fierce, relentless, ferocious-truly-
A wild tigress in battle-I do not apologize.
For the passion, the rage, the wrath and righteous fury,
Of this queen of paradise!

So much have I yet to tell thee!
And so little time-with aged hands-to be concise.
For I can never do justice,
To the magnitude, the splendour,
The magnificent presence-
The glorious and gothic grandeur!
Of the mighty queen of paradise!

She died-as she lived-
Without fear, shame or doubt.
I recall-with tears-her noble sacrifice.
Raised sword in hand-
And smiling eyes-raised to God-
Oh, Queen of paradise!

While yet a teen-the tall, golden-haired queen-
Picked up the dreadful dice-
Of war and triumph and slaughter and carnage,
Fair queen of paradise.

Her heart was always full of raging fire!
Her mind was often arctic ice!
For power-as always-gave harsh conundrums-
To the queen of paradise!

During a time of trouble and defeat,
(Which historians ever do rationalize),
There came a long-limbed, simple warrior girl-
From our country's cold north-
Who was soon to be-
The future queen of paradise.

She gave our lands peace and honest laws-at last.
And banished her enemies-who would-soon arise.
For as great in peace-as she was in war,
This queen of paradise.

Some-doubtless-will find fault with my long and varied record.
Since youth-I had the power-to memorize.
Yet-all and any action of this legendary woman-must be told-
And will be told!
For when I die-so dies also-the last living memory,
Of the queen of paradise.

The great are often much hated-hated for their strengths-
As well as their sins-and many are the lies-
Spewed forth like living, molten lava of
The fearless queen of paradise.

The earlier rulers-all rotten and corrupt-
With every unnatural, unmanly vice!
They were sent sailing-like chaff-before the wind,
By the incorruptible queen of paradise!

Honest, modest, virtuous-in private life-
She was-always dressing simply.
Like a huge elephant-compared to little mice.
Such she was-and such were the enemies of-
The queen of paradise.

Her death brought delight to many wicked men,
To the good-it brought a thousand aching tears,
Mournful lamentations and sighs.
For none could forget-the great, dizzy glory
Of the fallen-queen of paradise.

In her reign she saved so many lives.
And so many souls in battle-once or mayhap twice!
But the wondrous deeds-were all but erased-
Of the incomparable queen of paradise.

Brought low by horrible cowards and terrible traitors-
Who fill this wicked world like seething lice!
But long live the glory! And long live the story!
Of the queen of paradise!

A legend is a legend yet,
And a true legend never dies!
And the whispers and tales
And the ballads-soon re-grew-then blossomed-
Of our awesome queen of paradise.

So fierce-she was-in defending or in attacking-
But some scribes and scholars-verily-
Her mercy-do minimize.
(For they knew her not.)
They knew not-
The giving, loving, open heart
Of the living, loving queen of paradise!

Many of her followers were slain or put to death,
Through the rotting treachery-that dirty gold always buys.
Yet they all died-asking God for vengeance-
Calling out her name-and blessing-
The queen of paradise!

May this scroll of parchment-I write on-survive me,
Long after my blood and flesh dries.
Then my long life-is not wasted-
Nor the glory, in my youth I tasted-serving,
The queen of paradise.

Now my hair-once brown-is white and I see,
That a mortal cannot be a God-
No matter how he or she-vainly tries.
Yet I long and I pine and I wish
For the tumultuous, untamed days,
Of the queen of paradise!

Her name was spoken in whispers-in terror!
In adoration and adulation!

Thus how can I-a simple scholar-
Hope to analyse?
The riddle, the puzzle,
The darkly mysterious enigma-
Which was-the living queen of paradise.

Some have said,
She had magical, mystical, marvellous powers!
I cannot say for certain-no-but this I do not recognize.
For the magic was the beauty, the strength,
And the dauntless spirit,
Of the beautiful queen of paradise.

All honest men-who knew her-loved her.
All honest women too-I recall-
Her Majesty's last, triumphant horseback ride through, Karize.
The queen was sweet and mild,
The crowds were rapturous and wild,
O Happy queen of paradise!

When she drew her huge sword from the scabbard-
Raised it high-with a truly blood-curdling battle cry!
For her-a raging battle was a normal, healthy, exercise.
Then she led-her entire army-in person-
At full gallop toward the enemy-on Lunato-
Like a great tidal wave-surging toward the shore!
All conquering-queen of paradise.

Sometimes slightly wounded-
But never (miraculously), seriously.
Leading charges both on horse and foot-
She would fain monopolize-
The very battle front-her enemies often shrank back-
In sheer terror-at the mere sight and sound of-
The approaching-queen of paradise.

She once won a great battle-Tura-
In front of an erupting volcano,
And such a victory surely vies,
With the greatest battles of this world-
And won by-the jubilant queen of paradise.

Those that hated her were vain,
Selfish, corrupt, petty nobles-who suffer from
An all too frequent 'noble' malaise.
For they could not fathom, nor comprehend
The simple, innocent, power,

Of the loving, giving queen of paradise.

Her contrasts, her virtues, her vices,
Her faults, her strengths-
All this-I judge-mystifies.
But she was devoted to the poor and helpless-
And often showed great mercy to the wounded-
And bested in battle-
Thou much beloved-queen of paradise!

Impetuous, rash, passionate,
Impulsive, sudden, capricious,
Hot-headed-indeed, yea-all these-she could be!
As her record as a ruler-verifies.
But logic and calm, cool wisdom and clarity
Of thought-she had also in great abundance-
Felicitous, queen of paradise.

Her fierceness and wrath,
Her savage fury-her tempestuous violence-
Truly, her enemies sought to maximise.
For both the coward and the brave-
She sent so many to a very early grave-
Hence, the dreaded appellation;
'The Queen of Paradise.'

The myths, the sagas, the lays, the tales,
The epics of her dominion-
I could not possibly furthermore, aggrandize.
For she had kindness and vision,
She had innocence and laughter and hope,
Joyous-queen of paradise.

But she was too trusting,
Innocent, simple, open-childlike.
And many base persons, sought to capitalize,
From her generosity and bounty-
I saw this oft and warned her of this-
O, innocent queen of paradise!

To write on military matters is common.
Many do cogitate and theorize!
But to have the genius to wage war-
And always win-is most rare indeed-
Such was the genius-of the queen of paradise.

Posterity-perhaps-

Will judge her harshly or benignly-
As both time and deed-as all things-
Vaporizes or liquefies-yet-
Etched in bone-
Carved in stone-
One day will be fully known-
The sublime acts-
Of the immortal-queen of paradise!

Her enemies were many-her followers-
Many, many more.
The former-and I refute them-
Her fame-will seek to trivialize.
But none with honest hearts, minds and souls
Can ever doubt the truly epic deeds,
Of the noble-queen of paradise.

She killed the great general-Akumto-
In single horseback combat.
Not with a sword-but with an axe-
Held in a grip like a vice!
She beheaded him with one mighty blow-
His horse went galloping on with his headless body-
For many a mile-great queen of paradise!

But sometimes so girlish and simple and playful,
And in my mind and my soul-
One memory does crystallize.
The queen, softly, idly, singing a folk-song,
As she slowly rode her horse-one summers day,
Lost in her own mild, sweet, thoughts,
Thou tender queen of paradise!

A warrior, a woman-child, a mystic, a puritan.
Useless-almost-to categorize.
She cursed and threw out-two of her ministers-
With her own bare hands-
For accepted bribes-
Scornful, queen of paradise!

She was-alas-but nine and twenty-when she died.
Young, beautiful, resisting all
Worldly temptations-with which
Our sinful world always beckons and plies.
Yet even when betrayed and lonely-
Her thoughts were with her beloved people only-
And their sore distress and suffering-

Thou peerless, queen of paradise.

32pitched battles, she won decisively-
And 29 single combats-
In 12 years-and losing none!
I saw all her majesties victories-
They are fastened in sacred memory's ties.
And was there ever such an
All-conquering king or queen-anywhere-
As the salubrious, queen of paradise?

She was reigning queen,
From seventeen to twenty-nine-
She knew that men did not live
Only by meat, milk, bread, fish, oats or rice.
For holy was the soul-
And holy the many good works-
Of the queen of paradise.

I am aware that the mind can play strange tricks,
But my mind is yet clear, cool, calm, sober-
It neither deprecates nor beautifies.
Yet-you would not believe the glorious sight
Of our queen-riding forth-at noon-
On her ceremonial, golden chariot-
As all did call their love, praise and worship,
Their queen of paradise!

So many wicked untruths were spoken,
Written of her-since her death-
And be ye sure-none of this applies-
For none can know the dazzling,
Triumphant smile and happy laugh,
And the rapturous, joyous call to arms-
Of the invincible queen of paradise!

Often-she fasted, kneeled, humbly prayed-
And loudly called on God for guidance.
Too few-do realize. Her loyalty and love-
And devotion to all her people-
The devoted queen of paradise.

She was most exceeding clean and seemly.
Of habit and body-washed-very often-
As was possible while campaigning.
With her soldiers-she shared humble fare-
Meat, fruit, cheese, nuts, fish and honey lemon pies.

For she faced all dangers, hardships,
And triumphs alike-with her worshiping men.
Hail-thy triumphant queen of paradise!

It was said that she had dark,
Unworldly, supernatural powers.
Whereat, men-listening-were much amazed .
That she could cause ghosts and spirits and souls and parts
Of the dead-at her very biding-to suddenly materialize!
But this I regarded as mere foolishness, superstition
And fear brought on by the great awe-
Of the truly mysterious, queen of paradise!

She knew-all too well-the struggles, the sacrifices,
The efforts and perils of a soldier's life.
Who fights-and in the cold winter-freezes,
And in hot the summer-fries.
She protected them, cared kindly for them,
In every way she could-'twas by all admitted-
The caring queen of paradise!

But the savagery of our great queen in battle!
How shall I bear witness-or chroniclize?
With her huge, flashing sword-
Her great physical strength,
Speed, rage and fearlessness-
The terrible queen of paradise!

Astonishing indeed-at seventeen-
She could take the realm
And the heavy crown of duty.
War, violence, invasion-sweetness,
Tempest and calm-all this-
Like threads of music!
She could easily harmonise.
For few men or women-ever-possessed
The energy, daring, optimism or audacity-
Of the dauntless queen of paradise.

When she spoke!
Or shouted or called-
From afar-or near-to her soldiers!
Oh, she could win hearts, minds and souls!
She could hypnotize!
It-mattered not if-her voice was soft or loud-
Cooing-or bellowed-
All at once followed the war cry-

Of the calling queen of paradise!

Whence they come-
And whither they go-
All the joys of this world?
It causes one to philosophise.
And she?
Whither roves and wends,
Such a one-as she?
So naturally majestic-yet so often humble.
So destructive, so fierce-yet so gentle, and full of love.
So chaste-yet so full of violent and terrible passions.
Loving this life much-yet fearing not death.
Thou woe-assailed-storm-like queen of paradise!

She gave too much gold and alms, (some said),
To the poor, the lame and unfortunate.
From her kind and tender heart-and not-indeed-
As her critics claimed-to gain or win new allies.
For the multitude-willingly-pledged
Their troth, fealty-and life itself-to their protecting-
And avenging, soldier-queen of paradise!

Man is good-but also-doubtless-
A most sinful creature.
But our most glorious, queen,
Knew nothing-at all-of compromise.
'Do as I bid you all! Live in righteousness!
For it pleases God so much!'
Thus, spake-
The radiant queen of paradise!

In war, she was ruthless!
Brute, blunt, direct force-always-her foremost method!
But her judgement in legal matters was delicate,
Soft, tender, sweet, kind and very nice!
And when cruel, despotic, sadistic, callous kings
And queens-are all parted in contrast-
Behold! There stands-
The merciful queen of paradise!

'Victory-will go to the bold, the true,
And the fearless!' So said our queen-
'And see-all thou-my most brave, brave boys-
How victory now multiplies!'
For none could rally men-to attack-defend-
To conquer and gain much glory,

Like our beaming queen of paradise!

And battle after battle after battle she won!
Emphatically-often at great odds.
Through her genius and inspiration and her fierce
Readiness to pay-in war-the price.
'My most brave boys (she often so called her soldiers,)
And I can beat any and every foe in the world!'
Thus she told her men-thou, inspiring queen of paradise.

'For a battle is a lovely, glorious cake!'
Said she-
Smiling-like the great child that she often was.
'And we must-each and all-take for us now-
A very hearty, delicious slice!'
Such was the magnetism,
And simple, stirring, striving wonder
Of the miraculous queen of paradise.

To ignore her complexities-her range-her spirit-
Is tempting perhaps-but nothing simplifies,
The purity, the aggression,
The mayhem-the startling contradictions-
Of the unvanquished-queen of paradise.

Verily, man is a mixed creature.
Great good, great evil-dwell each-within his breast.
Yet nothing justifies-
The duplicity, the falsehoods,
The base ingratitude of those-who owed all to her-
The abandoned-queen of paradise.

Her soldiers, her army, her people were ever loyal-
It was a few wretched 'noble' families-
That began her tragic demise.
They lied, they spied, turned coat,
Gave assistance to our worst enemies-
And most foully betrayed her-
Sad, queen of paradise.

She would pat, kiss, praise, caress,
Whisper fondly into the ear-
And sympathise-so sweetly to her horse-Lunato.
Often-she rested her forehead against his-
Smiling-stroking his head-
She spoke softly to him-as to a beloved child.
"My horse, is the very best of all horses.

He has no fear in battle!" Said she.
"Never wavers, never hesitates-never shies!"
When Lunato died in the last charge-at her last victory
And her last battle-it very near broke the heart of
The queen of paradise.

When she died-five weeks later.
She was buried-on a hill-beside Lunato-
The weeping and lamenting in the land-
Was woeful-some say suffering purifies.
Yet I curse the day-the hour-the enemies-
The craven treachery-
That brought the end of
The betrayed queen of paradise!

'See! See how they run! See how they flee!
Like frightened, feeble sheep!'
Said she-at her last victory-Kotz-
Pointing with her sword-
'Now nothing will ever prise-
The victory-from our hands-my brave
And true and noble and lovely boys!'
Rejoiced-our queen of paradise!

Just-when she had won-and won all!
The cursed treachery began!
First by the unmanly coward and deserter
(Forever damned be his name!)-Turnise-
And then greed, sin, wickedness, envy
And incredible folly-all brought the fall of-
The soaring queen of paradise!

Before a battle, on horseback-more often on foot-from a hill-
(So that all could see her and hear her well),
She would give a speech-to her gathered army.
Her beautiful, most musical voice-
Her heavenly body and face-as she exhorted them-
Sometimes softly, calmly-sometimes with great animation-
To great deeds of strength, courage, daring, valour and fortitude-
Would utterly-mesmerize!
She drove them into a frenzy of battle lust!
They were eager-even if they were not before-to fight with fury!
Then all her men-young and old-timorous or bold-
Would happily fight, kill, maim, or die-that day-for-
The queen of paradise!

Her words were always natural, spontaneous!

Never studied-nor writ by other hands!
Her voice-poured forth like sweet,
Holy, honeyed music!
But such an effect she had,
How she could motivate and magnetize!
She could bid us to do the impossible-and-we did!
She told us that it was a great adventure!
Even at seventeen-she could-entrance us all-
By twenty-nine-she could well-nigh do it in her slumber.
Such was her spell.
No man, no woman, could ever match her for inspiration!
She was more akin to a Goddess than a woman.
"I will lead my beloved boys-to victory-
In the greatest battles in all the history of the world!"
Thus cried-arms spread high and wide-
The exultant queen of paradise!

The stormy voyage of her reign-
Whereof-the fame-was great,
A military tabulation of her deeds-all-testifies.
Yet how can I even begin to capture-
The pride, the joy, the thrill, the wonder and the rapture-
 In serving, in fighting-with and for-
The angelic queen of paradise.

She loved the simple things of life.
As much as she loved to elevate and spiritualize.
She encouraged acrobats, jesters, singers, dancers,
Rope-wanderers and magicians-all that would divert
And amuse her beloved people.
The queen kept two jesters at court-
For her own personal amusement-taking turns
To divert her-make her laugh-and thus make laugh-
The queen of paradise.

All children truly loved her.
Both boys and girls ran eagerly to her-
When she was near-
She would take a boy and girl at each village-
And let them ride slowly with her, for a while, on Lunato.
This was a great joy to the children!
Then she gave them honey cake and orange-water-
From her own flask-and after the ride-
Showed them her golden helmet, her golden shield,
Her golden buckled belt,
And her great, glistening, golden-hilted sword.
They were in awe-and asked her for advice-in war.

She told them to learn their lessons very well.
Obey their parents, be good, honest,
Truthful, and love God.
This was the simple, gentle, meek, sweetness of
The queen of paradise.

It was said by some-
And very widely believed,
That all animals and birds-
Fish-yea-even trees, flowers, plants and insects-
Secretly loved her-from afar.
That each and all would have done her bidding-
Obeyed all her commands instantly-
If she had only asked them.
Only she never did-such was her goodness.
This belief-I always much doubted. I thought it foolish.
But-all women loved her.
All honest men too-young and old.
She was as greatly famed for
Her kindness, truthfulness and honesty,
For her chastity-and the mystical power-which it gave her,
As she was for her bravery, fearlessness-and valour.
But her court and the noble families were rife,
With loathsome, writhing, crawling, twitching, undulating,
Maggot-like, traitor-spies!
And the higher and sweeter she rose-
The more discontented, dissatisfied,
And sour and sorry they were.
For as strong, powerful and mighty as she was-
She was almost without guile-
Thou pure and noble queen of paradise!

What is won over years-with lakes of blood-
And fields of sacrifice.
 Can be lost by one traitor in a trice!
And this sad, awful, terrible fact-
Soon spelt the end-
Of the tragic queen of paradise.

She rose so high-then higher still-
And then she fell-no danger she feared!
She threw back her head with glee-at all risk!
And she laughed aloud-at danger!
When she saw great armies arrayed against her-
She laughed.
So that brave men were much astonished.
And wise men were dumbfounded.

Then-she conquered.
Thus, she dazzled.
Adventure for her,
Was like-unto a zesty, needful spice.
Such she was! In good and ill-
In joy, in battle or in woe-
The intrepid queen of paradise!

She was usually magnanimous-to her enemies-
Once they were beaten, dead, crippled, helpless-
Or grovelling at her feet.
Without any fear-triumphantly beautiful-all this-
Doubtless-greatly her person-glorifies!
Like a mountain eagle-soaring-swooping-
Far above-to her true abode!
Such was the near incomprehensible-ascent-
Of our sweet queen of paradise!

Her sword-Thekla,
Her shield-Orsaf
Her helmet-Hemka,
Her huge belt with the great gold buckle-Demka,
Were forged for her by the peerless weapon-master-
Ulftok of Karthize.
He said they were his greatest achievement.
They were given to her when she was seventeen-
After her coronation-she was told to use them well-
To restore the honour, pride and glory of the nation.
This she did-many, many times over.
Each one was said to possess mystical powers.
No man-could in truth-say otherwise-
Given the queens, subsequent and utter, invincibility.
It was said that her sword, shield, helmet and belt-
Loved her with the passion of a husband for his new bride,
The tenderness of a mother for her new babe.
The loyalty of a dog for its new master.
That they would allow no sword, nor arrow, nor axe to harm her.
It was said that each could talk in whispers-
To the queen-or to Lunato-
To warn her or he-of oncoming dangers on the battlefield-
Such was the great love that animated their spirits.
This was believed very widely throughout the land-
And even more throughout the army.
I doubted it much myself-but no man can be sure of such things.
In truth-I and many others-saw her often before battle-
As she dressed in her tent-her long, white legs, barely
Covered by her armoured tunic-her long, white arms bare-

She would take up her sword and shield and helmet and belt-
In turn-and speak to them each quietly, earnestly and fondly.
She kissed them softly and bade them to do their
Business well that day-to carve and cleave for her-
And shield and protect her. She sympathised much with them-
And said she would lead them to another great victory,
Which she knew that they desired above all things.
She told them that after God, her country, her people and Lunato-
She loved them more than anything or anyone on earth.
When the queen died-
She was buried with her sword and shield,
Her helmet and belt.
That they might yet guard their queen-in Warkisto-
The eternal afterlife beyond-of all brave warriors-
Where she would and could claim the foremost place.
Such was the love inspired-even in fleshless, bloodless objects-
By the queen of paradise.

In action-in battle-
On frenzied battlefields-indeed,
Her genius-was brought into full flower!
Her mind-swift as an arrow-bold as a comet-
All this I fully authenticize.
The enemy would often-
Take to outright, panic flight-near falling over each other-
As they saw her, approaching-on Lunato-
Hearing her ferocious yet joyous battle cries!
Hewing down her assailants-right and left-with such terrible ease!
Many believed her to be of far more than mortal making-
So that they froze, fled, bowed, kneeled, eyes wide with horror-
Hands and limbs trembling with dread.
Surrendered-prostrated themselves-
In great numbers-crying in terror-to each other-
As they saw her approach,
"Look! Look! She comes-she comes-The Queen of Paradise!"

She killed the vile prince-Muntila of Fullize,
Who's wickedness was of malodorous fame.
He had slain upwards of three hundred of his people-
Many children included-for failing to cheer him-as he walked past-
Or for daring to criticize his person.
She did for him-in single combat-on foot-
Two armies-breathless, spectators.
The diminutive, feeble prince-
Disgusted all-as he sobbed, wept and shook with terror-
Crawled and rolled on the earth like a serpent-
Moaned, screamed and called for help-

He begged for mercy-he who had shown mercy to none-
As he faced the tall, mighty queen-who looked down at him,
With silent a scorn-open contempt-
As if it were beneath her to fight one
So craven and so puny!
Slew him-ended to his disgraceful career-
With contemptuous ease-and one quick, mighty blow!
Slicing his head in twain-
From the skull down to the jawbone.
I believe in truth-she was shocked by his cowardice-
It was strange to her-who was fearless.
She was all but ashamed-and indeed-very annoyed-
At having to challenge so pitiful a King.
She often complained about it-but had no choice-
Such-were the strict laws of single combat-among royalty-
In her time.
Such too was the bodily strength, swiftness, skill,
And frightening ferocity-
Of our modest, tender queen of paradise.

She built homes for the homeless.
Gave food to the hungry-
Much spring water to the thirsty.
Pure, chaste, noble love to the abandoned.
Much sympathy and assistance to the distressed.
Gold, diamonds, pearls to the poor.
She would comfort, help, rescue, philanthropize!
Verily! She loved all creatures and all living things!
Many a man, many a woman, many a child,
Many an animal-yea-many an injured bird-that she healed.
Many a fish-secretly thrown back into the water.
Many a thirsty plant and flower-
Sprinkled with spring water-by her own hand.
Many a tree-that she spared from being felled-
Because of her great love of trees-
Owed an eternal debt of gratitude-
To the soft-hearted, dulcet, angel-queen of paradise!

But she would suffer no rival on the field.
It was never known that she showed
The slightest fear or discouragement in battle.
When the odds were so heavy against her-
Where other men would have been cast down-
She was bore up by her joy in battle, by her love of life,
By the simple honesty of her nature.
'If the odds are heavy against me-it nothing signifies!'
Said she. 'The more glory, the more honour, the more joy,

I will have in overcoming all! Be ye all of most good spirits!
God protects the bold and brave and the true in battle!
Victory will surely be mine! Even, Lunato knows this!'
So spoke the queen-with a calm, happy smile.
And she spoke most true-for victory attended all of her labours,
Endeavours, toils and adventures in the field.
God or fate or luck-loved her-it seemed-like a cherished infant.
But against black treachery there was no such remedy.
This was the wonder and the woe and the way-
Of the queen of paradise.

She chased down
And killed the cruel, coward king, Karuta-
Who-revelled in strange perversions,
Loathsome, horrid rites and obscenities-
Dark, unspeakable doings!
Many said that he worshiped and was beholden to the devil!
He had killed peasants, farmers, hapless villagers-
Women, children, the muchly aged-over a thousand in all-
By firing them high from a giant, wooden catapult-
Newly erected in a field, near his palace.
This-his daily entertainment.
While he sat and ate grapes with his mistress's-
Convulsed with mirth by the frequently flying victims-
Flying sometimes-over a hundred feet in the air.
Many of his court took wagers
On who might fly up the highest.
These and other melancholy deeds-
Karuta-greatly delighted in-
Which make one blush for all humanity.
When the great queen was told of his conduct-
She was on military manoeuvres with her officers-
Practicing her skill at archery and javelin throwing.
She said not a single word. But-merely bit her lower lip-
And flushed bright pink-
Always-a sign of great rage with her.
The next day, she challenged Karuta-
To single combat-which he refused-
Bringing further shame on his despised name.
He then fled her in sheer terror-after losing a brief battle-
As all witnessed.
Such was her strange nature-which in danger,
In mayhem-which she loved-like a flower in sunlight-
It ever blossoms and thrives.
She had put his contemptible little army to rout-
(It was the easiest battle of her career.)
Then chased-in person-and slew the cruel king.

She said, he ran and hid everywhere a man could hide-
Under and behind everything-
With no more shame than a cat.
And in the end he was too afraid to fight her.
Until-he asked-that she would not use her sword on him.
She promised not to. Karuta-coward as he was-
Then quickly drew and attacked her with own his blade-
And she killed him-crushing his skull-with her shield.
How her soldiers roared with laughter!
This was the playful, lovely humour-
Of the blessed queen of paradise!

She killed the great warrior, Sulata,
A man of much size, bodily strength-in single combat-
After his most foolish challenge-watched by all in hushed awe-
Which our historian Merutat-so very nobly describes.
The queen fought him for more than an hour, at sunset,
Matching him strength for strength-speed for speed-blow for blow!
With sword and shield-till he wearied-and despaired-
And she slew him with great ease-
Splitting his skull diagonally in half-dashing his brains
On the earth like jelly-then she released his 5,000 slaves.
The queen of paradise!

She slew the defiler,
Deflowerer and ravisher of young girls-
The wicked, ugly, mercenary lord Bortar-who took
Pleasure In all manner of unmentionable abominations,
And delighted in most dreadful cruelties,
After she challenged him to single combat.
The legendary battle that followed was justly recorded-
By many notable witnesses and scribes.
The great queen never showed more courage,
Fierceness, speed, power or battle-joy-nay-even delight!
She decimated him-in three minutes-cut him to pieces-
He was helpless before her fury-she howled with triumph!
Hacked off his head-and threw it up high in the air to his army.
The queen of paradise!

She ended the two cruel and craven Kings-
Tirik-and Vorstak-both vile, sadistic, lazy, despicable-
In a famous, single challenge.
They broke the holy, sacred code of single combat-
By attacking the queen-at once-
In unison-one at each side.
Their own two armies, were appalled-
And-cried out; 'Shame!'

But the queen-nothing troubled-
Covered, herself with glory.
She dealt first-with Tirik-then-turned on Vorstag-
No need to mythologize!
She annihilated the pusillanimous kings-
Each guilty of most lamentable atrocities-
In less than two minutes.
Both wept in terror, begged for mercy.
She split Tirik's skull in twain-with an awesome blow!
Then destroyed Vorstag-roaring with rage
And battle-joy-as she did so.
Finally running her huge sword through
His neck-to the hilt-and twisting slowly it all around.
The two armies watched with silent awe.
Then cheered-the queen of paradise!

She slew the fat King Gunnit-
A man of bottomless vice-endless sin-
Who's every breath partook of some baseness.
Gunnit, boasted of raping twenty five,
Poor and defenceless young girls,
In a captured, enemy village-all in a single month.
None aged more than twelve-some much less.
The queen killed him with a noble justice-
That must tranquilize.
Gunnit-terrified-was far too fat to fight-or to run far or fast,
Hid in a remote village of his small Kingdom.
Disgraced himself yet further-
By hiding behind his wife, mother-in-law and servants.
He trembled like a wind-swept bush and groaned in terror.
But the queen finally cornered him-
Drew her huge sword, pointing it at him,
And told him loudly, with calm scorn:
"Base fellow! Your life of deplorable sin
And wickedness has found you out!
There is nowhere now to flee!
The trees themselves are ashamed to give you shade!
Five and twenty girls you befouled!
With your loathsomeness and corruption!
You most foul human fungus!
You showed them no pity-and I have none for such as thee!
False and abominable one!
You stink up the world-with your evil habits!
Your time has come!" Thus saying,
She thrust her sword fully through his fat belly
And carved a large circle In his flesh-
Then pierced up and through his chest-

While he screamed like a pig.
She pulled out her sword and he fell.
And afterwards, she washed her sword well.
The whole village gathered and showered her
With love and gratitude-many taking hold,
Caressing, blessing and kissing the hand that slew king Gunnit ,
And all gave her great praise and thanks.
For Gunnit was much, much hated.
Such, was the noble justice, meted out,
By the defender of all maidens,
All girls and women.
The queen of paradise.

In single duel-she killed the miserly-King Putolka-
Who revelled, shamelessly, gleefully, gloatingly,
In the misery and penury of his own people.
While himself-living in wild, extravagant luxury.
The great contrast, betwixt his immense wealth,
And his people's abject wretchedness seemed to transport
Him with a strange, fluttering, ecstasy and pleasure-
A singular exultation, rapture and very bliss.
It was said that he danced, skipped, laughed like a child,
Howled nightly-on the palace rooftops-
Screamed in joy-felicity, triumph-his eyes bulging-
When he bethought of his great riches
And his people's low indigence.
All of which, offended the queen's noble soul.
She merely shook her head without words,
On hearing of his conduct.
It was a battle-if such it may be called-
That men will remember-all of their lives.
The queen toyed with him for a moment-
He was quite paralyzed with fear-
His sword falling on the grass-from his limp hand-
And sticking into the earth.
She then cleaved his head off-with a huge lateral blow.
His head fell behind him and rolled down a long, grassy hill-
Happily chased by a dog.
Yet, his body stood there, upright, headless-for a moment-
Blood gushing like a fountain-from his neck.
She kicked his chest, contemptuously-
And he toppled over-to the tumultuous rejoicings
Of his own populace-who loathed him with a great loathing.
Then all bowed down to the earth.
With awe and love and devotion,
To the tall, blonde queen.
Such was the wondrous wrath

Of the queen of paradise!

There was a mad king
In a neighbouring land,
His name was Kermati,
Who's lust for wealth, gold, diamonds,
Pearls, rubies, sapphires and all manner
Of precious stones-was great beyond belief.
It was said-by spies and deserters-
That he had fashioned a statue of a beautiful,
Naked woman-with body parts, breasts-
Buttocks-of purest gold-and made her his wife-
For Kermati, loved her with surpassing ardour.
She was bedecked with diamonds and other precious stones-
Which formed her large, sightless eyes.
He partook in amorous, nightly congress-with her-
His great hope-that his seed might bring forth,
Golden children-which he could melt down-
With eyes of precious stone-
That he might pluck-and thus magnify his riches.
For as a man lusts after a woman's flesh-
So he lusted after all manner whatsoever of wealth,
Wherewith which to satisfy his concupiscence.
Such was the madness of the king.
For he taxed all his people beyond all endurance-
Proclaiming that all was his by Godly right.
Those who did not pay were cruelly put to death.
All their families-men, women,
Children and the elderly were horribly lashed.
So that the entire land was greatly cast down-
Longing and praying for salvation.
Now-a secret emissary was sent to the queen's court.
To tell her of the kings madness-his wife of gold-
The people's great distress and suffering.
They were willing-indeed most happy-to live under her rule-
If she would only kill the king-restore law and order-
Melt his gold-wife into coin coin-end the taxes-
And put his army to flight.
The queen-who was then enjoying
Her favourite cinnamon-honey cake,
(It was made with eggs, milk and whole flour,
Prepared by her personal cook-the loyal Kastrog-
Beloved by the queen-who later died in her service.
He also prepared her favourite drinks-ginger water
And orange water-which she took with her when
Campaigning-she belived them to be invigorating.)
She threw back her head and laughed greatly-

Collapsing on the throne-when she heard this-
Laughed most long and loud-to the emissary's surprise.
For she thought it was but a merry new jest put forth-
By one of her arch jesters-who were always hoping and wishing
To delight and surprise her and catch her unawares.
But when she was told once again of the golden wife-
Harsh taxes-and she saw it was not in jest-but in earnest-
The queen was greatly astonished.
"Such things cannot be!" She said simply.
For the queen taxed her land only lightly and with reluctance-
For which she was loved.
She resolved at once-Kermati to chastise.
The king was no fighter.
When she challenged him to single combat-
On a field outside his palace-as the whole town looked on-
He shook his head-refused-backed away.
He would not pick up a sword to fight her.
Instead he picked up a small child-held a dagger to its throat.
The queen desired that he put the child down. He did.
The queen then returned the child to its mother.
Then he picked up yet another little child
And held a dagger to its throat,
And again the queen asked him to release the child.
And again she returned the child to its mother-
As she did so-Kermati-seized and threw a spear at the queen-
While her back was turned-
Who span and caught it in mid air-with one hand-
Such was her speed.
Then she slew him-
With one sudden, savage blow-
Driving the point-of her great, sharp sword,
Down, through the top of his skull like a dagger-
As he screamed at the top of his voice-
So that the blade went all through
His head and came out below his throat.
He was dead within an instant.
The people cheered loudly-for Kermati-
Was held in high disgust and abhorrence.
All bowed down to the queen-who bade them-
Go about their business-happy and carefree.
Then-the queen-who greatly disapproved
Of all manner of harlotry and fornication-
Outside of the holy and sacred union of man and woman-
As being wanton and wicked and an offence to God-
Ordered that the golden wife be rendered down
And melted into gold coin and given to the people
In recompense for their hardships and suffering.

All the precious stones and gold coins-
All in equal measure-were distributed to every man
Woman and child.
For this she won their great, enduring love and loyalty.
They called her their true liberator
And deliverer from servitude.
Such was the justice-
Such was the love-
Of the queen of paradise.

Her most astonishing battle-
Though a miniature one-was the battle of Dontek.
The queen led a small, detached cavalry force-
Recklessly-as she later admitted-
Deep into enemy territory-without prior reconnaissance.
Caught by surprise-on the left flank-
Her force was one hundred-
And outnumbered five to one.
A desperate struggle followed.
We fought mercenaries on horse-of king Kula-
Who were renowned for their cruelty-
Notorious for killing and raping women of all ages-
Mercilessly slaughtering all children-both with great delight-
Two things the queen deplored beyond all measure.
It seemed our numbers would be overwhelmed-
That the queen would lose her first ever battle.
But just as we were falling back in great disorder-
The queen-who had been riding far ahead on the right flank-
Reared up on Lunato.
The queen commanded that we all stand our ground.
Then ordered a counter-attack.
Many of the troops were very young and much affrighted-
It being their first battle.
(Her veteran's soldiers on this day,
Were encamped, some miles away.)
The queen entreated, beseeched, implored
Them to fight harder. To follow her back into the fray.
She said she would rather die that day-than retreat.
She asked, pleaded, begged them to return to the contest-
Saying that she knew that the battle could yet be won-
Or she would not ask it of them.
She reminded them of their soldierly duty.
Of how their wives, mothers, fathers, sisters, brothers
And sweethearts were proud of them!
She said she would attack alone-if they refused to obey her.
Still, they would not stir.
Thus-she did attack alone-though her officers swiftly followed.

The queen charged and threw herself into the forefront
Of the maelstrom-the thickest of the fighting-with desperate courage.
Hacking, toiling-snarling, ferociously, ruthlessly, fearlessly-
Fighting, without the slightest regard for her own safety or life.
Lunato, lunging and rearing and kicking out mightily-
As a ship-in a tempest at sea!
She was surrounded by many fierce, brutal, loathsome enemies-
Who wished for the great honour and rewards,
Of killing or taking the famous queen alive.
She ended the lives of many of those who converged upon her.
The young army watching-was soon shamed into action.
Followed their queen-
And threw themselves back into the struggle with abandon.
The enemy broke and soon scattered and fled
In utter confusion and disarray.
Such was the terrible fear and superstitious dread,
Which the virgin queen inspired!
Our deliverance was a true miracle-and entirely due to her
Boldness and intrepidity.
When the day was done-a great victory-at great odds-had been won.
We had killed far more than we had lost-despite
Their vastly superior numbers-
And retained the field with honour.
All had covered themselves with immortal glory.
The queen-afterwards-only very mildly rebuked her troops-
With a broad smile-for their tardiness in following her.
A thing that had never, ever happened before-
Nor ever did again.
That day her boys became men.
It was a holy baptism.
She called them-her most brave boys.
Such a legendary leader in battle was-
The queen of paradise!

Thus, it came to pass-
Near the end of the great queens, glorious reign,
That she had her most legendary of single contests.
She challenged and fought-in front of two silent armies-
Prince Morkat-whom-though a great fighter-
Ruling a land almost as large and populous as our own-
Was a man of the basest imaginable proclivities!
Who happily boasted of his great enjoyment in raping
Upwards of 250 women-in a single year-and putting them
Into his personal bondage-
And killing fifty women for trying to escape.
Furthermore-he put upwards of 500-
Of their children into slavery-under the harsh lash-

In his mines-a certain death-for more than half.
He also had 100 children-innocent little boys and girls-
Put to death-for trying to escape back to their homes.
This sad tale soon became known throughout the land.
It is said that the queen-
Who was on horseback-wept openly-
When she heard the fate of the women and children.
And was most sore afflicted-
For she cherished all children, much,
And all womenfolk of all ages, much-
For she regarded herself as their
Sole, true champion and protector.
The queen then greatly desired that she might avenge them.
But this conduct also incensed our boisterous queen-
She was torn-rent with fury and righteous wrath-
And a terrible lust for battle!
I had never seen her so-berserk-before.
She screamed to the heavens in her scorching wrath!
She kneeled in prayer, then she rose and
She called on God to strengthen her arm!
Her very servants trembled as they went about
Their daily duties, lest the queen vent her fury and anger
By punching or kicking or lunging at them.
But this was not her way.
She smote only the strong-not the weak.
Only the powerful-not the feeble.
Only the wicked-not the righteous.
Five weeks passed between Morkat's,
Barbarous deed-and this famed combat.
But her rage did not abate.
She blushed, bright pink with fury-
When she first gazed at Morkat-
And dismounted from Lunato.
Her great blue eyes-usually so happy
And full of light-at once-
Grew hard and cold as diamonds.
She stepped forth, drew her sword,
And loudly, boldly called out a challenge to him in single combat-
As the two large armies at once formed opposing ranks-
Which he accepted.
Yet, the queen-perhaps-rejoiced inwardly
In having an opponent worthy of her.
The queen was tall. Morkat was taller-
Greatly famed for his bodily strength.
Such was the terror she inspired-
That few challengers, durst ever face her.
Battle commenced.

Nicholas Alexander Papantoniou

To the great astonishment of all-Morkat-
Was outfought, from the very first.
The queen was at full mettle-she fought
With a speed and delirious battle joy-that logic-all belies.
Snarling, snorting, growling with rage and fury.
The queen took the initiative and kept it.
They fought for a quarter of an hour-near sunset-
The queen always forcing him back.
Mighty blows rang out from both!
Never-had the queen fought more sublimely.
She was too swift-too fierce.
Too strong. Too fearless. Like a soaring eagle-she was!
One simple scholar has ventured-that mayhap-
Prince Morkat's, vital bodily powers-his essential liquids-
Had been too much reduced-spent too liberally and profusely-
Indulging-his unseemly, amorous appetites,
With a great multitude of women-
But this I regard as a most lame and pitiful excuse!
As do all, who witnessed this famous contest-
Morkat-in truth-was not yet thirty-five.
He was bested, vanquished-pure and simple!
By a stronger, quicker, younger, fiercer, braver adversary-
He scampered back, first in surprise, then desperation.
Groaning with despair,
She cut him ruthlessly, to ribbons.
At last-they reached the foot of a hill.
He was near exhaustion-breathing with great labour.
They yet traded mighty blow for blow.
Their huge swords, flashing in the crimson-golden light
Of the falling sun-that fell behind the huge mountains.
The two armies watched in a fascinated silence.
She backed him up, more and more,
Pressed him-hither and thither-
As an old master with a young pupil.
His weariness caused him to stagger-loose his footing.
The queen was greatly famed for one thing-
Among many others-that she knew not was fatigue was.
She never grew tired nor weary in battle-
Which is-in part-why all men feared her so.
For if they fought her-she would never grow tired-
Nor ever lose heart-
So that they were in increasingly grave peril.
The queen was never deliberately or coldly cruel-
For it was beneath her.
Nor could she ever abide cruelty in others.
Nor would she countenance any cruelty whatsoever, in her realm.
Even the slightest cruelty to domestic animals-

Or beasts of burden-filled her with a mad rage-
And was cause enough-for a personal or public censure
By the queen-for she always restrained her passions,
When dealing with her beloved people-
And was gentle and kind to them.
But now-she cut him deliberately-again and again.
Then, when he was almost too weary, to move-
She howled with fury and lopped off
His left arm-which carried his shield-
Just below his shoulder-with a single stupendous blow!
It fell with a clatter to the ground.
Then, she howled again with fury
And she sliced off his right arm-
Which carried his sword-just above the elbow.
It too-fell to the ground.
He screamed loudly twice-as she did so-
His stumps, moving idly, flowing, like two rivers of blood.
The queen then spake-breathing hard-but her voice,
Loud, clear and cold.
"Most vile one! Seldom-if indeed ever-has such iniquity
Dwelled in mortal flesh!
The clouds themselves-blush-for now giving you shade!
Disgusting one-I bear the foul, sickening stench
Of your sins-only that I may now bring them to an end!
This-I do-for the good women, you grievously, wronged
And have done most great injury!
For the innocent children-harmless, happy boys and girls-
You wickedly made slaves and also for those you cruelly slew!
One arm for each. I spare your legs-
That you may stand-while I slay you! Verily!
Woe, ever unto the wicked and sinful in nature!
For God will smite you by his-or by mortal hand!
I have no pity for such as thee!
Others would not show you so much mercy-as I have.
But enough talk! Most wicked villain-your time has come!"
And she drove her great sword into
And through his naked chest-
Twisting, turning it around all the while much-
While he screamed like a bird.
She pulled it out slowly and he was dead.
The two armies cheered her-
For Morkat was much more feared-than loved by his men.
The village came forth and rejoiced,
As the queen gave the order
To free all the children and all the women from bondage.
To distribute Morkat's great wealth between the villagers-
The larger share-going to all the wronged women.

Then she gave her sword to a servant
And told him to wash it well.
The village bowed down joyfully to the queen,
Who bade them all to rise-with her blessing-
And go about their affairs, untroubled.
Many hundreds of the women and children were weeping-
Such was their joy in being liberated and reunited-
All hugged and embraced.
Thousands upon thousands in the crowd-
Perhaps-upwards of twenty five thousand-
Who had journeyed from afar to watch
The much-awaited contest-
Then began chanting the queens name
To the heavens-in gratitude-for their liberation.
They chanted so loud, so long, with such solemn rapture.
Some said that the queen then wept-herself-
As she saw their great joy.
That she wiped her eyes many a time-
With the back of her hand-and thanked them-
And asked them to praise God alone-and not herself-
For she only did God's bidding.
Still-on and on they chanted her name!
She said to her servant;
'One day, when all the wars are over,
I too must marry and have children!'
Alas, it was not to be.
But such-was the good, pure, kind, gentle heart,
Such was the stark, dreadful, terrible retribution-
Of the queen of paradise.

The queen-and Lunato-both-greatly,
Loved the sound of the battle drum!
They fought, rode, moved-as one-soul-one heart-one spirit.
Neither knew what fear was! I remember,
The queen's greatest numerical victory-the battle of Kertrice!
The queen was thrown from horse-but Lunato-
Kicked and bit and reared and lunged and snarled at her foes-
Until she safely remounted-and patted his neck-
So much love had Lunato-for the queen of paradise!

She would ride ahead of thousands, at the charge.
A roaring joyously-sword-sky pointed.
And such a vision of beauty and blazing glory-
Many-indeed-would immortalize!
But for me-she was always a simple-honest-
Though-magnificent childlike-woman-
Glory, ever be-to the queen of paradise!

On wind-swept mountain, or on coastal shores-
She travelled-with her mighty army.
And she knew-all too well-what such power implies!
Never would she be false-nor lie, nor cheat!
But she would always crush and scourge and beat!
Her enemies-would grovel and bow down!
Before the queen of paradise.

Her battles were all victorious-her assailants-
At last-despaired of beating her-by fair means.
Misfortune-and treachery-she met with calm,
Noble courage-that truly sanctifies.
She was as brave, as virtuous, as truthful, as kind,
As tender and ever as generous,
When fortune smiled not on her-as when it smiled-
Unhappy, queen of paradise.

She was seraphic and adorable.
She could raise weary soldiers to conquer!
She said: "My most brave boys, are unbeatable!
If led by me-just as at they were Mutz and Torka
And Birg and Theta and Braice!"
And I see her-in the distance-on horseback-
Her victorious silhouette-rejoicing-beckoning-
Calling us to adventure and death or glory!
The bewitching queen of paradise!

When the bad times came to her-
Her enemies combined-in great number.
She came out of her royal tent.
She drew up her whole army-asked simply-
Who would stand by her? The army listened.
And so very few came the 'nays!'
And so very many were the 'ayes!'
For they were willing to follow her-
To death or to glory-hell or Heaven-purgatory-
Come what may-"All or naught!" they cried!
And how they fought and tried and strove
And battled and won and died!
For their own beloved, queen of paradise.

And though-in the end-she fell-
As fall, we all must.
What did it signalize?
No man, no woman can ever-nor will ever-match,
Those long forgotten deeds,

Nicholas Alexander Papantoniou

Those long forgotten dangers-
In those long, long forgotten days-
The days of the strange queen of paradise.

Such a woman-or man-is most rare!
That ever battles-never yields-and ever strives!
Such she was-that was the final miracle-
The queen of paradise!

The queen-to the end-never once gave up hope.
With dwindling resources-
Audacious, resilient, defiant, bold, fearless as ever-
She would organize, improvise, optimize!
Still, she fought with mad, relentless fury!
Still, she inspired incredible fear and dread-
Whenever she took to the field!
And still, she won many lightning, crushing victories!
But-sadly-shamefully-she was betrayed!
Stabbed in the back-not the front-by unmanly cowards-
Who owed her much-if not all.
Her beloved land was most sore afflicted,
Yet-its people-loyal, faithful, unyielding.
But to the end of her short life-
She remained quite unbeaten in pitched battle,
Unconquered in single combat. Unvanquished-
On the field of honour and glory and arms!
This no one could deny!
And it greatly, greatly consoled her.
Tall, proud, unflinching, fierce-though so betrayed.
Our queen was forever the same.
Forever invincible.
It was base treachery-perfidy-infamy-
Not greater might-that undid her.
"It is indeed, a bitter thing, to be so treacherously
Served and used thus!"
Lamented-with anger-shaking her fist.
The heroic queen of paradise.

I remember-a mother and daughter on the road-weeping-
Who had lost all home and kin, to an enemy raid.
The queen-then on horseback-watched and was much affected.
And it is far from my wish to moralize,
She dismounted, kneeled-hugging them both-
In a flood of tears and wails and sympathy.
And she cried;"Forgive me!"
Then she took them to live in her palace-
Gave them great riches-and fully avenged them.

The queen of paradise!

Often-in dreams-I hear-Lunato's hooves-
And a distant war-cry-echoing from the hills.
And I hear her name, shouted by many thousands,
Bellowed to the skies-loud-and thrice!
Then-I know well! She comes-now!
Her sword raised sky high-a laughing!
Her long, golden hair-flowing freely-to the four winds.
Her blue eyes full of light.
Her smile like the rising sun!
With happy and glorious battle cry!
To lead us-yet once more on-to do the impossible!
To conquest and to glory-
Bidding us all-always-always-
To despise fear-
To laugh at danger!
And to scorn defeat!
The queen of paradise!

The spirit of man is good and high-
Yet base and low.
Such a spirit-indeed-ever relies-
On those who would reach-span-stretch out-grasp-
Toward the distant stars-
That they may have the courage to follow!
As did she reach-and grasp-toward the stars.
The queen of paradise.

Her chosen high priest,
Oracle and alchemist-Balkavelo-
The highest of the highs.
Betrayed (it is certain), from jealousy-
His mighty mistress-the queen of paradise.

Her subjects had been enslaved once-
By foreign nations-in a tyrants guise.
Until freed by the boldness,
The daring soul and mighty body,
Of the queen of paradise.

To history's ears and eyes,
I say only one thing-
To those who would criticize.
That there once was a great warrior queen-
Whose like will not-again on this world-be ever seen.
She alone was called-with fear and with terror,

With love and joy. With blood and aches,
And tears, enchantments, raptures and magic and glory-
For all eternity-forever-the queen of paradise.

I finish.
I fear I have done but poor justice,
To her wondrous and all too short life-
Old and frail as I am.
For my powers are now too feeble to tell
Such a glorious tale!
And my hand is too clumsy, blunt and unpolished.
For-indeed-I lack all training in the nice, dainty rules of art.
For this I am sorry.
For I wished greatly-to do her justice.
But I tried my very best.

Once I was young.
I, Thesula, a humble scholar, from Karuntzi,
Attached to the court of the late, great queen,
At the age of twenty, in order to instruct and advise
The-then-seventeen year old-
Queen on matters, historical.

Unworthy as I was,
She took a great, girlish liking to me and my honest,
Impartial advice-as she-the bane of all royalty-
Was surrounded by flatterers and, 'yea' men, and foolish,
Obsequious, unctuous, knavish courtiers. I felt it my duty
To give the queen my best and wisest
Judgement and counsel. Soon she honoured
Me with her trust, confidence and affection
And drew me into her inner circle.

I remember at our first meeting, when she turned to me,
And asked for my judgement-on some trivial domestic matter-
Of which I had a good understanding.
I gave it bluntly-though it was quite contrary to the poor
Guidance-she was just then receiving.
She rose from the throne-her eyes wide-
Slowly approached me, impulsively threw her arms around me
And gave me a great, bearlike hug-nearly crushing my bones.
'Praise, be to God!' she cried,
'For an honest man and a wise scholar!'
(The memory brings fresh tears to my eyes.)
I was struck-as all were-at first meeting-
By her beauty-it was marvellous.
I never before or since-

Beheld the like.

She thence forward-took me under her royal wing-
And gave me protection-for at first-I had many enemies at court.
All seeking favour, preferment, gifts, boons,
And suchlike royal bounty.

Royal courts are most tedious things.
This one was no different!
It was-behind the elegant facade-a den of jealousy,
Envy, vice, scandal, deceit, wickedness and immorality.
All was very well hidden from the innocent, young queen.
I cared nothing at all for these vices. I merely wanted to serve
My beloved country and the noble queen herself-to whom
I was an utterly devoted follower-from the moment
I set my eyes on her.
I knew then-
She was one of God's chosen few.

She had a bewitching charm or enchantment-
Which defied all comprehension-since it was so
Obviously inadvertent.
Her beauty, childlike innocence,
Her warm spontaneity-mayhap-had much to do with it.

Many on first meeting-were greatly surprised-
By her kindness, sweetness, and natural ways!
This was when her mood was most relaxed and calm.
But when her mood was not merry but otherwise-
She stood still and tall and straight as a tree.
Arms folded-or her hands on her hips-one
Hand on her sword hilt-
And she frowned her terrible frown-
Or looked severe-
Because something was not to her liking.
Then near all would tremble.
Even if she spoke not so much as a word.

The queen gave me a high position at court.
I was to be titled, her, 'advisor extraordinary.'
Thus, I followed her everywhere-
In peace or war-for the next twelve years-
Until the day of her death.
I was but seldom ever separated
From her august person or her devoted personal staff,
And royal guard.
I saw, heard, witnessed all-advising when and where I could-

Riding into battle-with her-very often.
Inspecting-seeking out the truth-reporting in person to her.
She was soon pleased to call me her, 'sage'-
Or her, 'great sage',
Or even, 'O greatest sage!'
Far, far higher praise-indeed-than I ever deserved!
'Come, tell me! O tell me! O great sage!
What must I eat now for my dinner?'
She would say to me oft and then would laugh much-
Almost, collapsing with mirth-
Like the great, silly, happy, frolicsome, woman-child that she was-
When she was only calm and peaceful.
The, 'eyes and ears of our good queen-
In her bodily absence'-
It was said of me, by her staff, her personal guard
And indeed, by her wonderful, loyal, brave army.
All-heroes-to a man.

Numerous scribes and chroniclers,
Attack her want of judgement-
In that they affirm that she ignored,
The wisest counsel of her ministers.
But this-I attest-is of most doubtful fact.
Often her ministers advised her well-often they advised her badly.
For aught they advised, the young queen always decided herself-
Rightly so.

The problems confronting the great queen,
When she ascended the throne-would have baffled
The wisest and most mature and reflective of men.
It was a time of chaos and convolution-not peace and stability-
Wherein-she also might have had a still more glorious reign.
She was surrounded by ruthless, rapacious, barbaric enemies-
And she was then barely beyond her own girlhood!
This must always be taken into full account-when
Judging all her endeavours-both military and domestic-
Successful or otherwise.

Remember also-that she inherited all her wars-
She did not start them.
And though she enjoyed it so greatly-she often said-privately-
With a soft sigh-
That she did not wish to be always fighting.
She would rather build, improve, give help to the poor and needy,
And do good works and charitable deeds.
But the honour, the pride, the glory, the safety and security,
Of the nation was at stake.

And all must be done to uphold it.

For she was-at first-only seventeen.
Consider this most well.
As artless as her enemies were artful-
Untutored in the sad, false ways of this world,
As they were masters of it.
As innocent of all deception and mendacity and falsehood-
As they dwelled happily-in its very bosom!

That her natural intelligence, parts, hopes,
Instincts, were of the highest quality-
There is little doubt. But her education had hitherto-
Been-alas-most sadly and woefully neglected!
I remedied this as quickly as I could, with such methods,
As I thought best.
I found her to be a swift, tireless and surprisingly
Docile pupil-for she greatly wanted to gain wisdom-
And be a good ruler to her people.

Her love of her people,
Was a dominant feature,
Of this wonderful monarch.
She often spoke of it, sometimes-in tears.
Only her love for God exceeded it-she declared.

However, it would be in vain to deny that
Her natural talents-nature's very own bounty-
Her incandescent anger, rage and fury
At all falsehood, deceit, lies, wickedness, immorality.
Her immense physical and spiritual strength,
Her energy, bravery, incredible speed and confidence-
And utter disdain of all perils.
Her joy in battle and wonderfully great love,
Of victory, conquest, dangers and the heady thrills of armed combat.
Her childlike delight, in incessantly beating,
All her wicked, impudent, insolent, imprudent foes-
Who dared to challenge her supremacy in battle.
And her fierce, cold, pitiless, ruthless resolution-once resolved-
All these-were best directed to action, conflict, battle,
War and great events.

She has indeed been criticized by some,
For her inordinate love of war and battle!
But this is not at all to the purpose.
For consider this rightly and well-
That-had she even hated war-

Had she been an ardent pacifist-
Instead of a passionate militarist.
She must still, have been obliged to wage war-
Or else face a shameful surrender and an occupation
Of our beloved country to barbarian,
Uncivilized peoples-all intent on our nations, rape,
Destruction and ruin-all accompanied-with harsh reprisals
By cruel, revengeful armies-
And neighbours anxious to secure our deep
And precious gold mines in the south-the true source of
Our greater material wealth.
Therefore-I say-so much the better indeed-that she loved
War and battle with all her heart and soul-
And had a genius for it!
For she left a legacy in deed and song,
Which must never be forgotten!
Indeed, she once jested;
'War is the loving husband I never had-and I love it unto death-
And then even beyond!'

Though fierce, majestic and utterly fearless-
She was surprisingly sober, humble, moral-
And utterly upright-in her private life.
It was only in battle that she was transformed
Into a true Goddess of war.
Such was her character-such was the nameless awe-
Which she inspired in those who saw her in the flesh-
Or knew of her terrible-yet sublimely beautiful-legend.
I recall vividly the battle of Nemitza-where an entire army-
Upwards of twenty-nine thousand surrendered to her,
After the briefest skirmish-led by the queen in person.
The commander of their army-a man of experience
And repute-ran off headlong -even as he saw her-on Lunato.
This was the pinnacle of her awful and wondrous fame-
The truly preternatural dread which she awakened in all her foes.
It was indeed an amazing thing to see!
Thousands upon thousands of her enemies-prostrating themselves-
Kneeling-praying-falling-face down on the earth.
As she rode along their lines-triumphantly-on Lunato.
Paying tribute to her-loudly calling out her name-
Venerating her-laying down their arms, their every weapon-
Giving all homage to the great queen.
They seemed to stretch on for mile upon mile upon mile!
An undulating sea of bent backs.

She spent but little time in consulting
Astrologers, fortune-discerners, oracles and all manner of

Prognosticators and readers of auguries and omens-that hover
Around royalty like hungry bees.
The queen herself-in such matters-always preferred to rely
On prayer, devotion to God and her own great powers-wisely so.
I had but little faith or patience in such mystical
Wisdom-peddlers myself.
For I ever observed, that they spoke most vaguely and obscurely,
Were too much fond of wealth-considering their spiritual avocation-
And that they were right-no more often-than they were wrong-
And the merest fool could boast as much.
Or the humblest dice.

It is indeed a helpless thing to convey in living truth,
So many immense and astonishing events,
After so long from memory.
But I have tried!

And I hope-whoever reads this in the future-
If indeed anyone ever reads this!
Will ponder and meditate and reflect
And consider the life of this truly great-
And now-almost forgotten woman.

I can die in peace now.
For soon I will rejoin-
At long, long last-my lost queen.
And her abundant,
Faithful soldiers and followers.

As I pause,
I hear-distantly-the neighing of Lunato,
Rearing up-always-
Ready, eager, impatient,
To charge at the queens hated foes and enemies,
And put them all to flight.

So many have already gone before me.
I do hope to join them soon.
I long for it so. I yearn for it.
Truly, my heart has longed for it since the day-
That most terrible and accursed day-that we all lost her.
I am weary of life-without my noble queen.
Even as I write-I can feel the great queen, gazing at me,
Beckoning me-calling my name softly-once more-
Once more-and very soon-
I will hearken that call.

Nicholas Alexander Papantoniou

She was-I confess it now-
To God who-indeed-knows all-
The one great, pure, unspoken love and passion of my life.
I loved her the from first moment that I saw her-and that love
Has never faded, never dwindled, never dimed, never faltered
Never ebbed-in the least-with age.
It still burns most bright within me!
And I am now 98.
I have spent my whole life since, in mourning her.
Day by day. Month by month. Year by year.
I never married. I have no children. None will mourn my passing.
Better so. Mourning the beloved dead
Is a sad and terrible thing. This-truly-I know.

I have left some other scrolls and parchments and therein,
Lies a detailed record of the wonder and woe,
Victories and vexations, chaos and glory,
Of the madness, misery and utter magnificence-
Of her reign and realm and legacy.
A reign so rich in splendour,
So replete with great deeds,
So prolific, in noble quests,
So glorious, in heroic acts.
So wondrous, in epic conquests!
Let those noble souls-who seek the truth-
So long hidden among falsehood-
Attend these documents well.

Such untruths-put forth about her-in fulsome, great
Number-due to envy, jealousy, shame and wounded
Vanity-by those traitors, liars, fools, knaves, maggots,
Insects and scoundrels, who-in vain-seek to diminish
Her immortal deeds and conquests and justify their
Own infamy, weakness, cowardice, unmanliness and treachery!
Fools all-those-wretches-who can speak only ill of her-
Who was the most loved and hated, cursed, feared
And adored woman of her age and time.

I-Thesula-faithful and life-long servant
Of her majesty, do hereby solemnly swear that all
The above words are the truth-
To the very best of my knowledge-
And when in doubt-or where memory sometimes
Failed me-I have ever erred on the side of caution.

I hope these words,
Will live on in the future,

But I am past, making any further efforts-
As my strength is now fast ebbing away.

Thus, at last-
My long, long day on earth is done.
My queen, I come soon to join you once again,
Serve you once again,
And be nevermore, parted.

May the Almighty, grant blessings to our good, true,
Honest land and people-so brave, patient, sober,
And loyal-amidst dizzy success and stern misfortune.
And indeed, to all who live elsewhere,
For we are all his children!

I leave this document, to the inscrutable and
Unknowable hands-of posterity.
Farewell.

What were her deeds?
What were her virtues?
I leave it now for others-to surmise.
She was the greatest queen of all the queens-
She was the living nightmare-of men's hidden dreams!
Who's lustrous glory-through the ages-
Still twinkles, still glistens, still gleams!
She was our great and glorious,
And noble, young Queen, Agulanta!
The Monarch and Adored Ruler of Suramania-

And she was-
The Queen of Paradise!

November   23   1992   6.15-6.24.p.m

THRESHOLD

At heavens gates I stood,
Beyond the earthly smile or frown.
As if a clearing in a wood-
In space, nor green, nor red, nor brown,
Did interpose for ill or good-
At mornings glorious, lofted crown,
Or in hushed evenings close-it would,
When colours melt and tumble down,
Return to source-as but it should
Music in air-all falling mound.
But lifted its veiled, darkened hood
To light and knowledge, without sound.

June 15   2008   4.15-5.29.a.m.

THE INNOCENT LOVERS
OR A SONG OF THE OPEN ROAD

We have such a wonderful life,
Jenny and me,
Riding off into the sun,
Alone and free.
Days and days of fun,
I and Jenny,
Jenny and me-
Always on the run.

Always, on the road!
Always, on the highway,
In our Chevrolet we go,
For her way, is my way.
Jenny and I,
Me and Jenny,
In our roaring, soaring-
Jenny, by thy way.

We see sunrise, on the rockies,
And sunset, on the plains,
As we wheel by,
So many legendary lanes.

Four wheels rolling,
For my red-headed Jenny!
Romance is tolling,
For my blue eyed Jenny!
And then we go bowling,
Oh, my freckle-faced Jenny!
Forever on the move-big time-
My Jenny and me.

Tyres always spinning,
For my mighty Jenny!
Life always grinning,
For my slender Jenny,
Oh, great Lord above!
Thank you-for my winning,
My angel Jenny,
My pale-faced Jenny,
The wild, free dove of my heart!

In a drive in cinema,
My jenny and I.
In a drive in burger palace,
We sit and we sigh!
In a drive in sunset,
We say, 'my oh my!
Look, at all those colours!
They are the colours of Heaven!"

Oh, riding through the prairies,
I with my Jenny-in the blue.
Going through old Yellowstone-or Yosemite-
And she's laughing like a loon!

And the Badlands are good lands,
Jenny-when I'm with you,
And the keys of Florida-
Are the keys to paradise,
With you-my Jenny-
Sitting-so happily-by my side!

We drive in sun and rain,
In snow, hail and rainbow-
In dry-in windy-in storm and wet!
The Grand Canyon-was an epiphany-
We will never, ever forget.
And when we ride together-
On the endless road-
We don't ever worry or fret!

And our car is the mobile frontier,
On the American, dream.
And even from the distance,
We can see its shinning beam!

And the Rocky Mountains,
Do get me to counting,
The myriad joys of our life and path,
Right now-it's joy plus joy plus joy-
Minus sorrow-
You can do the math.

The sacredness of the dawn,
The noon, the evening, the starlit night-
Engraved forevermore, on our memories-
So many an astonishing sight.
And if I have done evil in my life-O my Lord,

I'm fixing to put it right.

Tyre-rubber always burning,
With my joyous Jenny!
On road-gravel always churning,
With my laughing Jenny!
And I'm always a-yearning,
For my sweet, kind Jenny,
Always, on the long, wide road,
Open-to the sky and stars!

And the whole, wide west-is blessed-
With abundant, glory and beauty.
And the huge mid-west-passes our own test,
Of high and holy wonder.
And the east is a beast of a feast-
For our eyes and ears.
And the Dixieland south,
Is the mouth of true joy,
And the north comes forth-
With pure truth, grace and light,
When I'm riding around with my Jenny,
They rise up-like a wave-on the horizon-
Crest-and unfold!

We have driven all over the U.S. of A,
All over America-
And what more can I say?
The land of the free-
Hasn't gone away,
And the home of the brave-
I reckon-is here to stay,
And so are we.

America, the beautiful
Hasn't taken a dip,
For we've seen it all-
And it's a real hip-trip.
Once-on the road-
We just let it rip!
We figure-this is all-our home,
God bless the open road!
God bless the highway!
And God bless America!
That goes for Jenny and me!

Nicholas Alexander Papantoniou

I guess some folks,
Think we're crazy,
Always driving, moving, searching,
Looking, roaming-
But we don't care if they do.
I want to shout it from a mountain top,
And whisper it, in the midnight blue.
For so many and many and many,
In this great huge country,
Love just like we do.
Yes, they do!
So innocent and true.

October 9   1991   9.4-9.10.p.m

ASCENT

I saw heavens glory glow.
The choir sang soft, in a heavenly hush,
Rich, melodic songs-that made my soul ache,
Building high, celestial, soaring sound-
My inner soul to wake.
And in my heart-I did blush,
For my sins and my sins-life long.

And I did weep bitter rain.
The tears stained my cheeks like blood.
Remorse did flow through me-
As oceans, fill the earth.

And I heard the trumpet sound,
The Angels-call my name,
And God's mercy and infinite love, I felt,
Releasing me-from blame.

I went up the gates,
Yet no ground to feet
And below and below-
I heard the earth retreat.

August 21   2011   9.8-9.19. a.m

THE NUMBERS

It got so bad,
Something had to be done.
Some wanted to stay-others wanted to run.
One stayed.
And there was one.

Many asked,
'Is it true?
And if it is-what to do?'
One thought.
And there were two.

It was night.
And the moon shone on the sea.
They stood-like wood-beside the tree.
One tried.
And there were three.

There was something,
That someone saw.
It was either a goat or it was a whore.
One fought.
And there were four.

Some couldn't swim and some couldn't dive.
Some could not sow,
And some could not scythe.
One prayed.
And there were five.

Some passed the time-showing card tricks,
Others were as friendly as
A dog that licks.
One wept.
And there were six.

Some asked,' Are we going to heaven?'
Others said, '20
Minus 9 is 11.'
One saw.
And there were seven.

Many shrugged and said,
'It's fate!
And how long do we have to wait?'
One trusted.
And there were eight.

Some said, there was a mysterious sign.
Others said it was even-
Visible on a vine.
One loved.
And there were nine.

Some said,
'The sword is mightier than the pen.'
Others said,' Are we going to heaven-and when?'
One sang.
And there were ten.

Some had been to Athens; some had been to Devon,
Some said,' 21 minus
14 is seven.
One raged.
And there were eleven.

One said,' Blame no one and don't blame yourself!'
Another said,
'To find the truth-you must look and delve.'
One looked.
And there were twelve.

ATHENS.
SEPTEMBER   14   1977

THE MUSE

All green the world,
All blue and gold,
As I run in rejoicing!
The rays of light and shine-all fill-
The secret dreams I sing!

'T'was on this world young lady,
I did spot your sequestered soul.
In deepest shade-curled 'mongst golden hay,
It shone like your hair-anew!

Oh, little blossoming testament,
Sweet, wild, mad flower of joy.
So young are you, with straw-like locks,
Will you hear my song?

Of amber and of crimson,
The world should glow for thee!
The universe-sufficient place-
For such a destiny.

Will you fly the world?
Will you dance on clouds?
And may I fly with you?
To the clear land you have journeyed from
And lay on the moss-alone-and woo.

You look back at me with your shinning eyes,
And a fun filled grin.
As I see it-I see your soul,
And the beauty-that is within!

Your secret is-you know-no doubt!
Joy was your morning gift.
If you guessed that they knew not life and love-
Your sandy brows would swiftly lift.

In your titter and chuckle and laugh I hear-
The melody of breeze and haze!
In your step and your stride,
I can see reside-
The beauty of golden blaze!

Dizzy, reeling through air and zephyr,
You lean your head back and softly listen.
The distant echo reaches-of immortality!

As you walk in shade and toss yellow hair-
Oh, Lord I can see!
The love in that smile-like the dazzle-
Would conquer all that be!

Eternal essence of power,
Of a skateboard and a light,
When I watch you dance and hum,
You make my will so bright!

Can I fly with you forever?
Your freckles would be my stars.
And journey through the sky-
The skies love-joined with ours.

A wonder of strange making,
An eerie plurality,
Born of trees and rivers,
Will blossom-eternally.

Your blue eyes, twinkle, sparkle.
A turbulent, fierce, living joy-
I have seen 'twixt dawn and sunset,
And nothing can-its power-alloy.

The silver green of trees and emerald leaf,
Evanescent shadows fall beneath.
The chequered grass,
And worshiping boughs await,
A glorious, incandescent-supremacy of fate.

A face such as yours has never been,
Each breath you draw-is joy.
So destitute of weakness,
'Tis power-without guile or ploy!

O mighty soul-the wind and howl,
Are tune to your spirit.
Prayer to the awesome, breeze,
You carry-in your soul.

You sweep all clear-before you,
The unworthy, may not hinder thee.
Some holy force-some grace transferred-
Heightened-a summit-alien-never seen!

Brush those locks from your eyes,
As you laugh and run,
Across, pastures-into dark woods.

The stream on its journey,
Through the forest of green-
Whisper-a secret understood!

This afternoon is thine,
Never was one so fine,
Will it not be divine-
This way?

Whatever thy girlhood glee,
When chasing the bumble bee,
The openness that you see-
Is day.

Waterfall and tranquil petal,
Your blue eyes wander-sometimes settle-
On a rainbow wound on a brook-
As you sit upon a branch.

Call them hope-Holy girl-
While the squirrels hop
And prance and curl,
In the midst of this mystic trance.

About you blow's the breeze,
Abandoned flow the trees,
Around you leap the leaves,
Against a sky-
So blue.

They seek to know the truth,
All things in nature would-
From anything so good,
And pure-
As you.

Jade and opal lane
I see.
A wonder I may never name-
In thee!

Could I ask the heavens,
Or the dreaming rose,
Or the colour-in the skies of this world-
For its truth?

The dark and weak-may not hinder thee,
Inviolable, are you from evil.
Free from the shadow of sin-golden maiden-
To pursue a path-of light-forevermore!

I cannot fall-for I have seen you-
And in my mind,
What I have known-always-is truth-
As I now find!

If only thee-alone-in dark,
Your spirit-true-would light,
All worlds and colours, scents and things,
A lane of love and hope.

You entered me as whole,
O my beloved muse!
And cannot float away.
Branches sway above
Your smiling, sky gazed head,
This summer's day.

The flowers will blossom through the season,
I'll lay and watch them for a while.
Before returning to other firmament-
In a young and awesome smile!

My little song is finished,
And yet will never be!
I only ask-may I take your hand-
In the presence of a tree?

I'd like to touch oh, pretty girl!
This thing, that fills you so.
This radiance-do not giggle-
Too young are you-oh girl-to know.

I'd like to hold your hand at sundown,
And in the shadows play.
I'd like to fly around and round,
So won't you tell your name?

December 18   2002   6.5-6.19.a.m

A PEACE OF ANCIENT GREECE

So go tell the Spartans,
That they will have their say,
And those who cannot speak-
Sleep in Thermopylae.

And go-run-tell Athens,
That the deed was done-
And those who cannot follow-
Dream at Marathon.

And go tell the oracle,
Such mystics are so wealthy,
For they learned their wisdom-
Gradually-at Delphi.

Then go tell the others,
At Corinth, Thessaly, Thebes-or Salamis,
That the Trojan War was started,
Just for Helen's kiss.

And go tell the Macedonians,
Of the coming roar,
Long, long after,
The Peloponnesian war.

And go tell mount Olympus-
Then let the games begin.
And they can play at home,
But, only play to win.

So go tell the Ionian,
And go tell the Aegean,
Then go tell the Mediterranean-
That glory lies in peace.
And you will hear the echo-softly-
That was ancient Greece.

Dec 15-19. 2010

THE FORTUNE TELLER
OR A MODERN GOTHIC TALE

Her name is Brigit Keller,
A middle aged woman-a fortune teller.
Is she only a clairvoyant,
Advising her wealthy clients?
Or is she a dweller-
In a dark, unseen and hidden world?
I cannot speak.
I cannot tell.
I cannot know.
Can you?

She lives in an affluent,
Old fashioned, leafy,
Residential neighbourhood in New England.
In a large, beautiful, colonial house,
Clutched by trellised ivy.
She herself is wealthy, respectable, cultured-
And-I won't say precisely where-
In truth-I do not dare.

She was once-obviously-
A very beautiful woman.
Still is-indeed-her thick, long,
Golden hair, now greying.
Her eyes-a striking, electric blue-warm,
But often also suddenly very cold,
Her complexion a fresh, healthy pink.
A native German woman-
Now an American citizen.
Her family-that is her grandparents-
Came here after the war.
Her grandfather-rumoured
To have been a top rocket scientist,
Smuggled over with
Werner von Braun's, elite group.
Her mother-a Prussian heiress-
Whose family had lost everything.
Her estate-formerly in east Prussia-
Now Poland.
Suffice it to say that the names
'Roswell' and 'Area 51',
Have been linked

To some of her grandfather's efforts.

Her voice is a deep contralto and husky,
With that charming, Teutonic accent,
(She had been educated as a child
With relatives, largely in Germany),
And she has a strangely lovely and winning smile,
That leaves you wondering all the while.

If asked about her profession (she often is),
She replies disarmingly,
"Why, it happens every day!
Death, murder, madness, horror, terror!
Just as life, joy, love, peace and beauty!
No matter what anyone,
Sceptic or believer can say-
It happens every day!
And that's the only way, it can be!
What more can I say?
I have a little gift perhaps!
And whether I assist
The police with investigations.
Or whether I help a wife
Contact a lost husband-
Or a departed relative,
Or a Mother, find or reach a missing child-
Whether I help a lady-or whether I help a feller-
I am only a simple, humble fortune teller!"

And she shrugs and laughs and goes on her way,
Leaving everyone smiling-almost applauding her.
She seems a very pleasant, nice,
Elegant and cordial woman.
But-afterwards-when she goes,
There seems to be a profound spiritual echo.
It leaves you feeling-
As though a ghost, had just walked quickly by,
I could not tell you why.

But I-and I cannot tell you
Who I am-by name-
For your sake-as well as mine.
I know.
Before I retired-
I worked for decades
At the state department-
In a fairly senior position.

I come from very old,
Very wealthy, privileged family.
I can say no more than that-
But-I have sat beside her.
And-I know.

When her icy blue eyes,
Look into yours,
You feel, the-oh, so quiet-
Opening of doors.
But-
What is beyond?

Does she really talk to the dead?
Can our minds truly be read?
Is there any truth in all-
That is whispered or said?

What one looks for-sometimes-
Dictates-what one finds.
Her clients all say, simply:
'Oh, she can easily read our minds.'

She has done amazing things,
In the here and now-
But nobody knows just how.

There is the, 'remote,' telepathy,
Poltergeists, telekinesis, palmistry,
Disturbing rappings, astral bodies,
The séances, the trances.
The strange, unaccountable accidents.
The sudden deaths.
The odd fatalities.
The rumours of-devil worship in her house,
And of conversations with-angels.
The miraculous healings through her
Divinely inspired-
Yet natural powers of thaumaturgy.

Some say she leads the celibate life of
A pure Christian woman and widow.
Others say that she is the head
Of a witches coven,
And regularly worships the devil-
During black mass,
And naked-presides and participates-

In diabolic orgies.
That she is aggressive
And sexually insatiable.
Now-are they really talking about -
The same woman?

And there's more.
Some say she accepts
All creeds, faiths, races, cultures
Alternate life-styles-with open,
Welcoming arms.

Others say, she is a fierce racist-a crypto Nazi-
With a scathing contempt for all, 'lower' races,
Black, Asian, Arab, Hispanic, Jews.
That she has often spoken-
In private, of the, 'great dangers',
Of miscegenation-in the modern world.

Her defenders say that this
Is utter nonsense- just gobbledygook!
A conspiracy of lies-
Put out by her many bitter, twisted and jealous enemies.
It is-indeed-a really, 'dreadful calumny',
And an, 'appalling defamation',
Of a such a good, kind, generous,
Compassionate, profoundly gifted,
Deeply spiritual-and yes-even noble woman-
Whose charitable works and donations,
Are both generous and exemplary.
And so it goes-endlessly.

Is she a modern-day Medusa?
Or a spiritual mother Teresa?
Is she a joy or a horror seller?
I don't know, you don't know,
No one really knows enough-
About-the fortune teller.

But no!
It can't be true-you say!
This-admittedly,
Strange and mysterious-woman,
Is obviously so very well educated,
Erudite and civilized! So punctilious,
Well mannered and gracious!
So well groomed, well dressed and so charming!

Pay her a visit-
Take tea with her-see for yourself!
Get your very own consultation!
See, the lovely, eighteenth century furniture.
The antique ornaments.
The old paintings on the walls.
The tea-served on Georgian silver.
She is the victim of arrant gossip-
Nonsensical, parochial superstition.
Just like the luckless witches in
New England-of old-at Salem.
And then she is so very attractive
Youthful looking and-
Well-yes-sexy-In a very understated,
Unfussy, unselfconscious way.
She could be-potentially-a magnet for men,
But she never flaunts, it or courts it, or even
Seems particularly aware of it.
Said to be, extremely wealthy-she is without doubt-
One of what they used to call, 'The Beautiful People.'
One of what they used to baptise, 'The Jet-Set.'
She is rumoured to have friends and clients
In very, very high places!
Movie stars. Sport stars. Opera singers.
Heads of state. Even-some say-royalty.
Her demeanour is modest, quiet, dignified, very serious.
Conservatively attired-yet-lovely,
Glowing, radiant with health.
There is such an honest, earnest, thoughtful look
In those big, blue eyes.
But they seem to be searching your soul-
As she looks directly at you.
Perhaps they are.
As if she can know everything-just everything-
About you-within seconds.
Perhaps she can.
As if she can do anything-at all-she likes-
With that knowledge.
Perhaps she will.
Very deep bosomed. Very full bottomed.
Tall, straight, slim-marvellous posture.
Walks-head high-like a born queen.
Full of vitality, with a crisp, energetic,
Decisive, no-nonsense, matter-a-fact manner.
No! She is just the local woman of mystery.
Every town has one-at least one.
Trace her ancestors back all through history.

Through the age-old tragedy's of her sistery.
But what I'm looking for is-
Her story.

She has her attackers, she has her defenders.
And how the rumours got started about her-
Nobody quite remembers.

Whether abrogating, unearthly, mystical powers,
In her quaint, old fashioned, tea-time hours-or-
As a guide-an amanuensis-to and for the departed.
But don't go looking for answers-
You'll be sorry-you started.

Planchettes and Ouija boards?
There are tales by the hoards.
Crystal balls?
She has them on shelves on the walls.
Tarot cards?
Oh, they stretch out for yards!
Crystals and quartz,
Of all different sorts!
Fancy checking out your Karma?
She'll give you the facts-without drama!
Just give her your palm,
Then try to stay calm-
As she reads.

One woman-during a séance-
Was said to have fallen from her chair.
Rolling around, gasping,
Licking the marble floor.
Barking like a dog.
She stayed that way for an hour.

There are rumours of an elderly lady,
Who-during another séance-saw or felt something so terrible-
That she lost the power of speech for five weeks.
She didn't have a stroke.
She just went to the fortune teller.

Another client-a young woman-after a routine consultation-
Found that for seven hours, she could speak fluent Greek,
German, Swedish, Spanish, Italian, Dutch and French-
And she joyously rushed around town, sought out and talked,
To as many foreigners and tourists, as she could while her
New and inexplicable, facility lasted.

Some say it's just,
A kind of, 'super-astrology', she practices,
Oriental and occidental-
With her, 'foretelling' –premonitions-or precognition.
She fortells.
There is no question-in my mind-that she can!
If only a tenth of the stories attributed to her are true-
It would still be quite staggering.

But is it possible-to see the unseen?
To know the unknown?
To believe the unbelievable?
To look into other dimensions?
To know both here and now and the beyond-
The finity and the infinity?
To unpeel everyday reality-
Like it was a banana skin?
To just casually-
Open a door to eternity?

She hears, 'Voices,' 'spirits',
'Holy presences,' reported by some or
'Unholy vibrations'-noticed by others.
She contacts departed, 'souls'.
Clients who have suffered physical, 'convulsions',
Or broken out in terrified screaming,
Or shrieking fits or fainted,
During séances-are too numerous-
Eyewitness testimony-too prolific-to recount.

Most of the stories sound so,
'Far-fetched', and unbelievable-
And so-frankly-utterly preposterous-
So redolent of the loony hatch,
That they are widely dismissed-
Quite without checking.
Tall tales-verging on acromegaly!
But are they all really so unbelievable?
Are they?
I wonder.

I first met Brigit Keller-
Back in the wonderful summer of 1977.
I was then a fairly bright, young thing,
In the state department.
Back in the days, when the cold war was still

Chilly enough to make one shiver-just a little.
It was in Washington,
At an official state department reception.
I'm not even sure how she was invited-
Must have been some
V.I.P.'s guest-or date.
There was some soft, mellow, 'disco' music,
Playing in the background.
I remember-as I shook her hand-being struck
By her intense, glowing, shining, blonde beauty-
She was quite a stunner!
Probably, the most absolutely, stunningly,
Beautiful woman I'd ever seen.
That includes several famous movie and T.V. stars-
I remember, she had such a lovely, warm, exciting smile!
A friend of mine told me-
When I later that evening-
Enquired about her-
That-young as she was-
She had proved, 'outstanding',
At detecting Russian, 'sleepers', in the U.S.A.
On account of her 'very special gifts'.
When I asked him-
What just exactly, these 'gifts' were-
He said he really couldn't say more-
It was 'classified'.
He did tell me though-in confidence-
That she, 'possibly',
Had links with neo-Nazi groups,
In West Germany, Denmark,
Norway, Finland and Sweden and elsewhere.
And, 'contacts', in almost every major European country-
From Holland and Belgium to Italy and Greece-
Including the Baltic states-and the Ukraine-
Although, 'of course', it was, 'highly probable',
That she had simply,' infiltrated', these groups-
In order to spy on them-for the West German
Government-in order to track down,
'Right-wing extremists'-
That was the rumour.
She was being, 'Loaned to us,' for a while.
'Also-if you like-she can read your palm-
She's very good! Too good. It's a little creepy!'
My friend told me with a pained look.
I remember-being quite impressed
On hearing all this-
Characteristically, ambiguous-information-

It was a portent, of things to come.
But I also remember, thinking-
How strange it was,
That such a very beautiful,
Young, fresh, dynamic, long legged,
And obviously sexy woman
(Even though, I was then
A relative newlywed, very happy-
And absolutely adored my wife),
Should give me such an odd,
Uneasy, chilling-spooky-
Yes-even a frightening feeling-
When I looked right, deep into her,
Large and intensely blue eyes.
I actually do believe I shivered!
I was not usually the nervous-
Or intuitive type.

But enough of my old reminiscences!
Another former client, claimed-
Absurdly of course-
After a money disagreement with her-
That her, 'astral,' body entered his room
While he was asleep-
By' seeping' under the door-
'Tapped' him on the shoulder-
And laughed-right in his face, as he awoke.
The next day-
While walking across a street-
He was struck by a speeding car-
Teen-age, drunk driver.
His back was broken-
And he is now permanently confined-
To a wheelchair.

It is said that a twelve year old girl
Who had a violent argument,
With the local psychic-about her dog-
Chasing the fortune teller's cat
(Strangely-a white cat.)
Went-on the day after the altercation-
Into a deep coma, for a full month-
For which the doctors could do nothing-
Before suddenly recovering-
As suddenly-as she had succumbed.
Her dog-a day after her abrupt recovery-
Was run over and killed-

By a beer truck.

Another story I heard just recently.
A young man-
Who didn't pay his consultation fee-
To the fortune teller-was eaten by a bear,
While on a camping trip-
On the weekend following
His delinquent payment.
His-or what little was left of his
Horribly, torn, mangled, savaged body-
Was found the following week,
By a group of girl scouts.
But bears were normally quite unknown,
In the thickly wooded area,
Outside the town-
And the police were mystified by it.

Is she just another happy medium-
With a flair for self-promotion?
Or is there a more sinister cause,
That she serves-with such devotion?

Some say she destroys faith in the faithful,
Others say she reaffirms-
Restores faith in the faithless.
Some say she has caused total madness-
In the perfectly sane,
Others say she has brought total sanity
To the perfectly mad.

Some say she has materialized the devil himself,
In her own living room.
Others say she has spoken cordially with angels,
In her kitchen.

Some say she is
A haughty, vindictive, concupiscent
Autocratic, malevolent woman.
Others say she is remarkably
Down to earth, level-headed,
Self-deprecating, kind, sympathetic.

Is she a glorious life-affirmer?
Or is she an all-devouring death-kneller?
Do ponder this-I beg you-before you see,
The fortune teller!

It is said that one private detective,
Several years ago-
Who shall-again-remain nameless-
Whose investigations got-a little too close-
To uncovering the truth,
Was taken into a psychiatric ward,
Screaming and raving-
He declared that he was being followed
By a giant black spider-
Which no one else could see-
About the size of a large dog.
He had first noticed it,
He informed the doctors,
When he saw the huge black, hairy thing,
That morning, climbing
Up the foot of his bed.
And it then proceeded to
Follow him everywhere-
In the streets, in supermarkets,
In a darkened cinema,
In every room in the house-
Including the bathroom-
In his office, in the garden, even his car.
He begged the doctors,
And nurses to help him.
He said some local fortune teller,
Had, 'set' the spider on him
To drive him crazy.
Naturally-the doctors medicated him
And he remains in a secure unit
To this day.
And-
He's quite mad.

It was also said-
Ludicrously, one might comment-
That she was responsible
For the death of one man,
For whom she had an unspecified grudge,
By causing a sledge hammer to 'levitate'
From someone's tool box-
And travel onto a highway-
At very high speed-for several miles-
And strike the windscreen of the man's car,
Causing a crash that proved fatal.

But all this couldn't possibly
Have anything to do with the fortune teller-
Could it?

Another individual,
An ambitious young, Wall Street banker-
Had some sort of 'fiscal' dispute,
Or, 'conflict of interest',
With the future predictor-and later privately claimed,
(Although, he seemed perfectly rational
When I spoke to him.)
Seriously, he claimed-
That late one moonlit, summer night,
While he was walking the short distance
Home on an empty, suburban street,
He heard a quiet, husky chuckle from above.
He looked up.
He swears that he saw the fortune teller-
High above him, perhaps thirty, forty feet.
Suspended in mid air-
Hovering, floating or flying,
Slowly, smoothly and silently,
Peering down at him,
Arms spread out-like wings.
She called down to him;
"I'm watching you! Wherever you go!
Remember that!"
She chuckled huskily-again-he said-
With great amusement.
Terrified, he ran inside his house.
Locked the door. Breathing hard.
And went up to his room.
To his amazement-he saw her, floating,
Right outside his bedroom window-a mere yard away.
Arms still spread high, wide, wing-like.
Looking at him-
Expressionlessly-through the glass.
"Ach, ya! I'm watching you. Always! Always. Always.
Just you remember!"
She repeated and floated or flew away.
He watched her for a few seconds-then-
So-he claims-
He fainted.

The man settled his 'fiscal dispute',
On the following day-very much
In the fortune tellers, favour.

He did not mention the previous
Evenings somewhat 'elevated' encounter-
Nor did she.

Well now, this is utter nonsense, of course-
True, the man quite readily passed a polygraph test,
Which I absolutely demanded that he take.
I can't account for that-I admit it, frankly.
I do believe that-he believes it all.
But what you see,
And what you believe you see,
Are often not the same.
I'm inclined to think that someone
At his office that day-on her orders perhaps-
Tampered with a beverage of his-
Slipped him, a hallucinogenic.
And he had a 'bad trip.'
Oh, it happens.
Sadly, surprisingly often.
It was known to happen in counter-espionage.
I remember hearing amusing stories,
When I was in the state department-
When things were a little bit quiet in the office.
We'd all have a good laugh at such anecdotes.
Russian spies or red Chinese tails,
Given a little something extra,
In their coffee or tea or milk-
The good old spoonful of opiates.

It is also speculated-
By her detractors of course-
That she 'killed' her own husband.
By hypnotizing him-one night-
After a furious argument-in which-
She shouted accusations, curses
And reproaches-at her spouse.
Sometimes in English,
Sometimes in German.
Slapped him. Scratched him.
Punched him. Kicked him.
Bit him-drawing, blood.
Threw things at him-
And finally-just by using her eyes,
Staring-at him-from a mere six inches away-
She put a powerful, hypnotic-mesmeric-
Or trancelike spell-on him.
Ordering him to drive for hours-

Still under the influence of the spell,
And ride at high speed,
Off a cliff into the stormy,
Foamy, cold Atlantic.
(Several witnesses saw it happen).
Saw-the car going over the cliff.
Thus-she inherited all his money.
And also punished him-
For cheating on her-with another-
And-much younger-woman.
The 'other' woman-by the way-
Also met with a fatal car accident,
Shortly afterward.
Crashed, headlong, into a car driven
By a young man-who at the time-
Was smoking marijuana.
Both died instantly,
Over two thousand miles away-
In sunny Malibu.

Her apologists say-on the contrary,
She was absolutely heart-broken,
When her-ten years younger-
Husband-Hermann-
A former Olympic weight lifter-
Quite inexplicably took his life-by going over a precipice.
She was wracked by guilt- 'Wept, profusely',
According to friends-and was at a complete loss,
To account for his sudden, strange suicide.

There was another odd case, once.
But very different.
Twelve year old girl, Susan.
Shy, pale, freckled, blond girl-
Very keen on music-very talented-
But lacking all self-confidence.
She wore teeth braces, eye glasses-
Extremely timid and introverted.
Saw the fortune-guesser,
Only one time-with her mother.

It was reported by five witnesses,
That on the day following her solitary visit-
And for exactly one week-
Whenever she played the guitar-she would, 'levitate',
Very slowly, until she was about a foot
Above her chair-and for exactly forty-five seconds-

Was totally suspended in mid-air.
But only, when she played, transcribed, early Beethoven,
Pianoforte, compositions.
(Apparently-this was the music that she took
With her-when she saw the for-teller).
After levitating,
She would descend, gently, gracefully, regally,
Back down onto her chair.
She would be in a deep trance-all through-
And she had no recollection of it at all.
While levitating, and playing her guitar,
She repeated,
Over and over, in a quiet, toneless, flat voice;
"Susan is high, Susan is high, Susan is high!"
Over and over,
Till she stopped floating.
No one managed to take a picture
Of her doing this.
They said, they tried,
But the camera malfunctioned-
Every time.

Naturally, no one believed the story!
That's hardly surprising.
I'm not even sure that I do.
And I mention it only for the completeness
Of this narrative, and my absolute desire
To give all the information I have about this woman-
However strange or peculiar, bizarre, disturbing,
Or remote from everyday experience-
It may be.

But all the five witnesses-
Four teenagers, one adult-
None of them inebriated or 'stoned'-
Swore on their lives,
That they saw it happen-the levitations-
On seven, separate occasions.

The fortune-describer,
During her only meeting with Susan,
And her mother,
Had casually remarked;
"This girl has a high soul!
She will certainly rise in the world!
I see her rising, very soon!
With her music and her guitar."

Coincidence?
Maybe.
Maybe-not.

The most notorious case
Was that of a client,
Who one morning, went into work,
And had smuggled an axe into his office-
And during a weekly staff meeting,
This man, described as a,
Quiet, phlegmatic and a, 'real low key guy'.
Suddenly-during the staff meeting-
He screamed at the top of his voice,
Stood up-brandished the axe-
And proceeded with
Savage speed and violence -
To kill five of his colleges-
Three men and two women-
Beheading one of the women-
Before being shot dead,
By a security guard.
He had seen the fortune-looker,
On the previous evening,
And according to one source-he
Looked 'pale, flustered and crestfallen'-
As he left her house.
In this case-as in all others-
Without exception-
She was at a public engagement-
A very worthy, liberal charity.
Seen by dozens-
At the time of the attack.
She always cooperates fully and graciously
With the police and authorities-
Indeed, she gets on quite famously with them.
Knows all their names.
Their wives names and their children's-
Even their dogs or cats.
Gives them all free consultations-and, 'advice',
Because she, 'admires them so,' and is, 'so very grateful'.
She's a true pillar of the community.
A genuine bedrock of our great American society!
And she always-always-always-
If and when necessary-
Has an absolutely air tight alibi!
Rest assured!

So many fumble,
Tumble, into her grasp,
And there is no escaping her clasp!
So don't stumble to your doom-
As you stagger-
Through the murky gloom.
Helpless-as a baby-sleeping,
Blissfully in the womb-before the abortion.
Too many mumble, bumble--then crumble to perdition,
Some say its nonsense-or just superstition-but-
Don't make her leave her room-or tomb.
And cast her spell or spells-on you!
And don't, whatever you do,
Don't ever underestimate, her-'powers'-
Simply, because you're an agnostic, secularist,
Atheist, or 'post-modern',
Or, 'too scientific'.
What?
What's that you say?
It's too late?
Oh, you poor, sad, stupid fool!

The facts are very plain,
No matter what-or whom-you blame.
Many of her former clients,
Most of whom-were far too pliant,
Are now insane.
And it cannot be too often said-
An awful lot of them are dead.

Her eyes tell her all.
The inner eye.
Middle eye.
Beware the eyes.
(They see right through you.)
Cyclops eye. Third eye.
Spiritual eye. Serpents eye.
Give it whatever name you like-
But believe it.
I know this for a fact by personal experience,
And genuine, prolific, eyewitness/ear-witness-testimony.
Which-once more-I will not go into.

For simply-far, far too many-
Who have finally guessed the truth-
(Whatever it may be) -

Are now too scared
To ever speak out-publicly.
Off the record-perhaps.
On the record-no.
Many-less prudent-have already
Been silenced-
Forever.

For we must remember the light
That knows no darkness.
And beware of the darkness
That knows no light.

She might well read your tea leaves,
But no one really, believes-
That's all that she can do!

Then say a prayer or a psalm,
Before she reads your palm!
In the shadows,
In the shadows, she dwells.
In the secret, mysterious light
Of the human soul.
In the hidden world-the dark maze-
Of the human subconscious.
But what part does she play
In the shadows-what role?

So take this warning and heed it-
And it might keep you safe.
Most who were lost-
Had no protection-at all-
Some-not even faith.

So chant your mantra!
Or sing a hymn
For she can kill you-
With a whim.

She knows the how,
The why, and the when,
But is it a strange power-or is it Zen?

You may not believe,
What you see.
But is it magic-or E.S.P.?

Nicholas Alexander Papantoniou

Without wings,
Without a broomstick,
On suburban, moonlit skies-she flies!
What manner of woman is she-
And in what divine,
Or devilish guise?

But-who can part her mystic veil?
What man would not quail-
Would not falter and pale?
For fear the fortune teller-
Would tell his tale-
Of doom.

Do you see her?
Eyes so blue,
Hair so blond,
She smiles.
Her wizardry is so
Consummately honed,
But are the real believers-
Or-disbelieving sceptics-conned?
No one-for certain-knows!
For those-who of mystery are fond-
Who saw not the enigmatic cloak-
Which she somehow,
Mysteriously donned-
Find the answer!
But with angels or with demons-
Does she bond?
And all her miracles, all the cures,
All the magic-
Without a wand!

Now, they do say,
There was a man once,
Who wanted to tell all-
The troubling tale-of the fortune teller.
One day-they say-he went deaf.
The next day-he went blind.
The next day-he was paralyzed.
Although-just for a while!
Just as a warning-
Not to tittle-tattle-
Not to be a tell tale,
Not to be a tale bearer-
Not to tell-anyone-anything at all-

About-
The fabulous fortune teller.

So-is she a nightmare bringer,
Or is she a fear queller?
Take a chair, if you dare, at the lair,
Of the fortune teller.

It is said that her
Immensely wealthy grandparents
Were fanatical Nazis.
Her grandmother-Anna-a tall, blonde,
Aristocratic beauty in her time-
In particular-
Was believed to be a devoted adherent
Of the Third Reich.
Knew the Fuhrer personally-
As a teenager-before the war-
First met him at Bayreuth-
With her family-and-
As a very old lady-
Living in retired comfort in Milwaukee-
Lamented the, 'lovely, glorious old days',
Referred to him fondly as
'Dear Adolf', and said he was,
'Very nice and charming and polite', to her.

But another source claims that this is
'Probably nonsense'-
And that the grandparent's loyalty
Was to the patriotic,
Prussian, militarist, Junker tradition-
And the former Kaiser-
Whom the family also knew personally-
(They had met him once at a reception-
Before the Great War-following an army parade in Potsdam,
And he complimented the fortune tellers,
Great grandmother-Hedwig von Keller-
On her blonde beauty.)
And that-to the contrary-
They absolutely, 'worshiped ',
Kaiser Wilhelm the second-
The last Kaiser of Germany and the-
'Great, glorious days',
Of the German empire.

After emigrating to the U.S.A.

The family-discreetly-dropped the noble-
'Von', from their name.
Although this source confirms-
Both her grandmother's-
And great grandmothers-
Striking good looks-
And states that going back further
Her ancestors were among
The founding members
Of the Thule society.

It is believed,
That some of her other relatives-
During the war-served in the Waffen S.S.
One of the fortune teller's uncle's,
Kurt Ludwig Keller,
Was said to be a member of the fanatical
And fearless teenage tigers,
Of the legendary-doomed and daring-
12th S.S. panzer division, 'Hitler Jugend,'
Which fought heroically at Caen-
And sacrificed itself-in the summer of '44
To cover the retreat-
Of the escaping German army,
At Normandy-by keeping the jaws-
Of the, 'Falaise gap', open.

Another and older relative was rumoured
To be in the famous-or infamous-
'Totenkopf', or, 'Deathshead',
3rd Panzer division.

Still another young relative, died,
'Doing his duty', in Egypt and Libya,
In the illustrious Afrika Korps,
Of the Wehrmacht,
Led by the renowned
Field marshal, Erwin Rommel.
This relative, fell-heroically-at Alamein.

Rival sources claim that the fortune teller-
And her many relatives now living in Germany-
(The Keller's or von Keller's are a very large tribe,)
Like most modern Germans-
After two generations of
Specific, 're-programming'-
Were now essentially, pacifists.

Her war time relatives-
Whatever they did or didn't do-
Were simply German 'patriots'.
'Doing their duty,'
During a dreadful war.
No more than that.

There are eyewitness accounts by those
Who claim to have seen her 'astral body',
Said to look like a leaking, 'vacant vapour'-
Or her' ectoplasm', or 'spiritual protoplasm'-
Escape her body, during her trances.
And, 'waft up and down and around the room,
Very quickly and smoothly'.

She is said to possess quite astonishing powers
Of prophecy, precognition or divination.
That she can find, 'anyone, anywhere, anytime!'
And had been paid, 'immense sums', for her services,
By both various governments-and by private-
And extremely rich families.
She has, 'saved the government millions',
In surveillance, ransoms,
Detective work and labour hours,
Over decades by helping in
'Hundreds', of open and closed, kidnap cases-
Which she had 'always'
Concluded -'satisfactorily'-
With victim returned home-
Alive and safe.
And the culprits behind bars-or dead.
Mostly dead.

A number of families,
Without surplus wealth-
Have spoken of the 'immense help',
That the fortune knower provided-
Free of any charge-
 'Pro bono publico,'-one might say-
In returning their loved ones.

I spent a few months,
Some years ago-
During a sabbatical-
Chasing down, many of these cases.
Several-in the mid-west.

One woman, whose only child,
Had been kidnapped.
In utter despair-
Sought out-the fortune reader.

Within twenty four hours,
Her young daughter-
Was returned to her-
Alive-in perfect health.
This woman, declares,
That the destiny diviner-
After merely looking
At a photograph of her girl,
And 'feeling and touching and sniffing'
An article of the child's clothing-
(An old blouse), sat down,
'...And went almost at once,
Into a spooky, trancelike state and spoke gibberish.
I know it wasn't German-I have an uncle who's German-
On my mother's side. It was just plain gibberish...'
And through, 'some weird, remote telepathy, she '
'Tuned in', to her daughters,
'Distraught and anxious vibrations '.
Took about an hour.
Then-she woke up suddenly-called the authorities.
The child was found-exactly-
Where the fortune watcher had told them.
The mother-a charming,
Honest woman-speaks of-
Well now-I do happen to have the letter
In front of me, and-I so quote:
'...I sure do owe Mrs Keller
A debt that I can never, ever repay.
Thanks to her incredible, heaven-sent gift-
Whatever it may be-I have my little girl back!
My daughter and I will always remember,
This wise, sweet, kind, wonderful,
And enormously spiritual woman-
Mrs Brigit A. Keller-with the deepest joy and truest gratitude!
She refused all my many offers of payment!
She said that to see our joy in reunion-
That was all the payment that she required!
If only there were a few
More like her-in our world-always doing God's work-
On the side of the angels,
Against Satan and all his worldly devils-
And foul followers-

Just doing good works-like Mrs Keller-
Without any desire at all for reward-I do believe-
This world would-sure as hell-be a better place!
May the Lord bless her! '

Such a heartfelt endorsement,
Requires no further comment,
I think-from me.

And-in fairness-I should point out-
That there are those-
Some with unimpeachable credentials-
Who insist nay-swear-
That she has 'brought about',
Sudden, immediate and astonishing 'healings',
For which the medical fraternity
Could offer no plausible explanation-
And for which-the recipients themselves
Were 'eternally grateful'.
I have seen-signed declarations to that effect
By many of the parties involved.
And I have spoken to some of them myself.
They're 'for real'.
At least their testimonies are.
What the facts are-I won't speculate-
But there you have it.

Now, lest I be accused
Of a lack of neutrality-before I continue-
Let me pause-let make it quite clear-
That it is neither my intention
To weave a panegyric-
Nor to rush to condemnation,
(Let us be ever mindful of Salem),
In the case of the singular woman in question-
But to serve the great-
And often neglected-interest of impartiality.
Yes. A dirty word these days. Ah, I know. I know.
In the strange, polarized, world and society,
We live in now.
Impartiality-a tarnished word-perhaps-
But it is essential to all
Clear human thought.
The pros and cons
Must always be reckoned-impartially,
Without fear, bias or favour-
For all, and by all, and with all.

That's the deal.
It is-after all-the commonest of human failings-
That we are all essentially reductive
Of things of which we disapprove.
And utterly expansive-of things of which we do approve.
Impartiality-that sacred, 'neutral zone',
Of the intellect-is sometimes very hard to find.
But it simply has to be there.
Or we all collapse into factions,
Bias, disunion and labyrinthine chaos.

For let us remember-
In full and sober humility,
Which of us-if we had only those
To condemn our doubtful deeds-
And none to praise our good actions-
When the scorecard-of our lives is tallied up,
By our recording angel-or celestial stenographer-
Which of us-would ever reach,
The pearly gates?

Having said that-
And I could certainly say nothing less-
I now resume my tale.

One man after an interview
With-you-know-who-
Was found by neighbours in his bedroom,
Crawling on all fours, a piece of raw meat
Hanging from his mouth.
He believed himself to be
A wolf-a merciless, lycanthrope-
He explained-In one of his rare and
Dwindling moments of lucidity.
He is currently in an institution.

Another woman,
Claimed that she saw a ghost,
Outside her window-staring at her-
For exactly five minutes-
Each night-for a week.
This was after a brief and incident free
Consultation with the supernaturalist.

There was a very strange case,
About twelve years ago.
Involving a young woman-Sarah Howard.

I don't scruple to use her real name, since the whole
Affair was widely reported, at the time.
Having seen the fortune-searcher,
With no apparent ill-effects,
She-Sarah-two nights later-developed a,
'Split personality.'
She claimed that she was, Amy Schultz,
A fourteen year old, high-school girl from
Minnesota, who was-she said-kidnapped,
Brutally raped and murdered in 1972.
Subsequent investigations proved-astonishingly-
That there was an Amy Elizabeth Schultz-
Of Grand Rapids, Minnesota, who disappeared
In the spring of 1972-without a trace.
In an interview with the police, 'Sarah/Amy,' broke down
And sobbed as she described the ordeal of her rape
And murder. I've seen the transcript of the interview
And I don't doubt its veracity.
The details are harrowing, heartbreaking.
All the more-for coming from a naive and innocent
14 year old girl, who was looking forward to seeing,
'The Partridge Family,' on T.V. that evening and had
A big crush on David Cassidy.
The fortune glancer-was contacted-by the police-
And went to work. She told them-a mere day later-
The location of the girl's remains. Amy Schultz's parents-
Were both dead-but her older brother and sister both alive
And grateful for closure-no matter how painful.
The fortune teller also gave the police, the locations of six other
Bodies-all teen age girls-all victims of the same man- who went
Missing between 1970-1975 in the Midwest.
The killer was still alive. The fortune teller told the police-
Where to find him.
He was picked up and is now serving
A life sentence, without parole.
As he was being taken in,
A large dog-leaped at and so savaged him-that he required
Sixty stitches on the face, neck and chest.
The dog-the puzzled owner said-had never previously
So much as growled at anyone before.
The killer-by the way-now in his sixties-was a text book,
Sexual pervert, deviant and sadist-
Addicted to violent pornography.
Sarah Howard, lost her, 'split personality,'
As soon as Amy's body-was found.
But her own, underwent a metamorphosis.
She began howling obscenities late at night. Sleep walking.

From being sexually inhibited, She began joining in group orgies.
This lasted only around six months,
Then she suddenly became herself again.
That's it.
I can find no entirely rational explanation for any of this.
But these stories proliferate-the closer you get-
To the fortune teller.

Yet another woman, claimed,
And she passed a polygraph,
Which I privately arranged-
That the medium turned her
Hot chocolate into mud-
And then back into hot chocolate.
This woman has since
Left the locality.
My belief was that she told the truth-
To the best of her knowledge-
But that some kind of cup 'switcheroo'
Or 'con' was involved.
But of course-
That's just my opinion.

However-just wait while I light my pipe-
And I'll tell you one of the strangest stories-
I've ever heard, in all my years
Of tracing and following the life
Of this unusual and remarkable woman.

It is alleged,
That one ambitious,
Small town magazine reporter-bored-
With the petty, monotonous trivia,
That he was asked to cover-as an-ahem-a 'gossip guru',
Decided to become a, 'deep undercover', journalist.
In search of an 'awesome, original story',
On the fascinating subjects-
Of 'modern-day devil worshlpers',
'Modern day neo-Nazi's', or
'Modern day witches,' he had hopes of-
Winning a Pulitzer prize,
For this ground breaking piece of dazzling,
Reportage on these most atavistic subjects-
All happening here and now-early in the 21st century.

Now, hearing rumours about
Our peerless prognosticator-

He rented a cheap room near,
The fortune teller's, home.

He began posing, as a 'recreational' Satanist-
(Whatever that may be.)
Or 'part time', neo-Nazi,
(I should point out that-there
Are two opposing versions
Of this story-which-In itself-
Strikes me as highly dubious.)

It is claimed-the now
'Secret' journalist- struck up
A casual friendship with the necromancer-
Was invited to-tea for two-
And testing the water early-he-
Began blasting, raging and lamenting,
Deliberately for more than half an hour-
At 'all the damned, coloured races-swamping-
Taking over America!'
And 'all the damned, mincing,
Faggots, queers, fairies and sodomites-
Totally ruining-our American culture!'
All of which-apparently,
Far from shocking her-
And although she said nothing-
Seemed to have delighted-the clairvoyant.

He was-on the strength of this-
Invited, a week later,
Into her 'inner world'.

Now his, 'deep undercover gig'- grew stranger.
The first version of the story tells us that,
He accepted her invitation-very happily.
But once there-he was told to bow down,
Kneel, before her.

He was asked to take a 'blood oath'
Of loyalty to the great ' Aryan and white race.'
And swear absolute loyalty
And fealty-to her and to-
'The white race's, glorious destiny,'
This vow-he was told-must be kept-
On pain of sudden death.

He was told to swear,

To be eternally faithful-
To the 'ceaseless battle-
Against all other, 'inferior' races,
Who actively seek-to destroy the white race-
To pollute it, poison it, undermine it, to drag it down,
Sabotage, subvert it, ruin it-wipe it out.
Spiritually, intellectually, culturally,
Morally, physically,
Both openly and secretly through,
Cultural weapons, those great Trojan horses-
Of, 'political correctness',
And, 'affirmative action',
Or, 'positive discrimination',
And through the, 'masquerade of multiculturalism.'
The main weapon-she said-
Chosen to bring to pass-the total
Extinction of all the indigenous white
Europeans and their descendants,
Was the, 'Biological warfare'-of interbreeding.
This-he was told-was now causing,
The slow, 'silent', and unreported, genocide of the white race.
This prolific programme, of mass miscegenation-
Whether-done deliberately or not-
It was mostly deliberate-hardly mattered.
The result-the aim-the intention-was always the same:
White extinction.
All the while-politicians and a liberal media-
Deliberately ensured, that the white race,
Slowly, inexorably, sleepwalked to its oblivion.
Never, ever forget-he was told-
That the inferior races hated the white race-
Because of its long and unchallenged supremacy-
Were jealous of it. Would always combine together against it.
Would not rest until all whites-
Were absorbed or extinct or grovelling slaves.
Many already were.
This was the battle.
It was a battle for the survival of the white race.
All whites could fight in this battle-
Individually or collectively.
There would be no help from liberals.
They were all pansies and masochists.
He must swear to fight on,
In any and every way, until
The ultimate triumph
Of the superior and invincible
And noble, white race.

On his knees before
The fortune teller,
He so swore.

Also included-
Was an obligation-
To have sexual intercourse with her,
During, ritual ceremonies.

Now, the second version of the story alleges,
That she then led him down to her,
'Secret chamber', in the cellar-or basement-
(In one story it's the cellar,
In the other it's the basement.)
Full of Nazi, memorabilia,
Guns, flags, uniforms, swastikas,
Jackboots, helmets, belts, daggers,
Decorations, photographs-one of-
A U.F.O. or flying saucer-
That the Nazi's were supposed, to have invented,
Which her grandfather helped build-
Based on something-called, 'Vril' power.
'And a lot of creepy, witchcraft stuff!'
Devil worship books. Occult lore.
Old texts on witchcraft from the middle-ages.
Books,' with lots of weird, spooky illustrations!'
Books on materializing dragons and unicorns,
And turning people into werewolves.
Magic spells for causing sudden death.
Accidents. Curses. Various, strange evil spells.
Magic incantations, which turn serpents,
Bears and birds of prey into assassins.
A learned, 19th century work, written in French,
On how to turn any domestic dogs, cats, squirrels, birds,
Spiders, house fly's, and mosquito's,
Into loyal sentinels, servants or spies.
A slim book, written in German,
On how to make enemies-
'Dissolve, melt and disappear.'
A very old, ornate book, written in Italian-or Latin-
On how to levitate weapons; swords, hammers, dirks,
Axe's, mace's, shields, chain-mail, knives, forks and nails.
An English book on proper and correct etiquette-
For formal ceremonies-at a witches Sabbath.
A book on how to make objects simply disappear.
And a book on how witches must always
Evade detection and discovery.

A book on a secret spell-
Only for the most advanced of witches-
Granting-the magical power of flight.

The journalist, also stated,
That there were literally
'Tons', of gold bullion or bars,
In the cellar, hidden under floorboards,
Which she told him, had been smuggled out by
Her grandfathers, relatives in the S.S .
It had been ransacked from all over Europe.
It was worth untold, millions, she said.
She was not even quite sure how much it was worth!
She showed him one of the gold bars.
He noticed how heavy it was.
(Ingots we trust.)
She told him, she used the stolen, Nazi gold
To finance her;
"(Expletive deleted), pansy Liberal, charities!"
And then she threw her head back
And roared with laughter.
"I use it, to give to all the, "(expletive deleted), faggots",
And all those, "(expletive deleted), blacks and kikes and
(Expletive deleted), gooks, chinks and wogs",
And those, "(expletive deleted), bloody Spics and Arabs."
She thought-it was a marvellous irony.

She demonstrated her own power –
To our fake journalist-
Who was, 'astonished',
Materializing-out of thin air-
A blue frog, a pink rat, a yellow spider
A red tortoise and a diamond beetle.
Then she made them disappear.

In her closet-
She actually had-a real, full, human skeleton-
She said she, 'could it bring to life!'
And, 'make it dance.'
She used it for various
Mundane spells, day-to-day, little curses,
Incantations, for scaring people off, and dull,
Humdrum, witchcraft doings.
And-also-she had a large collection of whips-
Which she used-she said,
'On those who disobey me!'
At which point-she is supposed

To have turned-
And given him a big wink.

He went along with all this-he had to-after all.
What choice did he have?
He was already-in too deep.
Including-both versions do agree on this-
Sleeping, with the pneumatic occultist.
He said that sex with her was, 'incredible'.
'Totally out of this world.
I never knew such incredibly,
Intense sensations or such strange, blissful pleasure!
She was a wild tigress in bed. Full of animal lust.
A sexually, voracious woman.'

The journalist, noticed,
Even in the ecstatic throes of passion,
A small, strange-looking, translucent, blue disc,
Resting on her dressing table.

However-a month later-
Attending a devil worship, ceremony-
His first and only-
The undercover journalist-
Was so horrified by what he saw-
That he vomited.

His hair, which had been dark brown-
Turned white-within days.
Not grey-but white.
He aged-in appearance-perhaps
Ten years-in one week-due,
Apparently-to pure terror.

He committed suicide-
Two weeks after this ceremony.
No reason given.
If there was a suicide note,
I have heard from one source-
A now retired police officer-an old friend of mine-
That there was-but it vanished.

It is conjectured-that he realized
His 'cover', was 'blown',
And he was terrified at the prospect
Of the fortune tellers, certain retaliation-
Now particularly-that he had

Broken his, 'vow' to her.

He died in hospital,
As the doctors tried to revive him,
Having taken a massive overdose-
His girlfriend had arrived, just as he was
Taking it-called an ambulance-but too late.
His last words were to a nurse:
"Please-for God's sake-please-
Don't, don't, let her-get me!"
He said-eyes wide-
Looking terrified-according-to the young nurse,
Who naturally, assumed that he was talking
About his girlfriend.
Then he collapsed, dead.
He was twenty five.

Needless to say,
The fortune teller's allies, state
That this is all-the, 'sick and sad product of
A deeply troubled, disturbed mind
And an overactive imagination.'
And they could be right-or wrong.
Apparently-this man-did have
A brief history of substance abuse-
Hardly unusual these days-and when younger-
He also had something of a drink problem.
Drugs and booze problems,
Don't naturally or easily inspire
Confidence in one's, veracity.
And as a child-it came up later-
He frequently made up wild fantasies,
About his life-but, then again-many children do.

He supposedly kept a journal of all this-
All his meetings with the seeress-describing-
His intoxicating but exhausting, sexual encounters.
And other strange, supernatural happenings and whatnot.
Very detailed, precise, meticulous.
Times. Dates. Places. Events. Names.
But the journal also strangely disappeared-
After his death.
All the facts can really support-
Is that he was-a suicide.

As for the suggestion that she is a
Reincarnated Uber-queen of 'Nazi's',

Her champions-state that she frequently,
Gives' big, big', money to African charities.
To Jewish, Arab, Chinese, Malayan,
Japanese, Indian, Pakistan, Bangladeshi, Sri Lankan,
Indonesian, Mongolian, Latin-American, Aboriginal,
Native American, Turkish and to Eskimo charities.
To the homosexual community, to AIDS charities-
And how could any true, self-respecting 'neo-Nazi',
Possibly do that?
It's a good question.
Now, I checked. She has certainly
Given a great deal of her own money
To all of the above-
And several others besides!

By the way-her cellar and attic-
And under-floorboards were thoroughly checked
For rodents-some years ago.
There was no gold.

There is another theory-
That the 'Neo Nazi' and 'Satanist' stories were all
Initiated by a certain mysterious 'rival' psychic-
Some years ago-in order to destroy her professional reputation.
No one knows for sure-who he is-or what happened to him.
He seemed to disappear-about ten years ago.
He once described himself as her 'nemesis.'
But perhaps-it was the other way round.
Probably, we'll never know.

Anyway-seizing on her obvious German ancestry-
Opportunistically-with all the residual prejudice,
And connotation that it brings-he promulgated-this weird tale.
Her advocates state that the Nazi/Satanist,
Rumours are malignant lies and total, blatant,
Monstrous and-one might say notably prurient-fabrications.
They say this 'rival psychic', hated her, because she
Spurned his numerous sexual advances-in addition-to his
Desire to usurp, her thriving psychic, 'business'.
I heard this notion from more than one source-
Confidentially and I believe it to be credible.
Although, I don't go so far as to say it is fact.
It would certainly explain the nightmarish,
Gruesome, highly and oddly sexual nature,
Of some of the narratives.

So-as always-two rival, competing, versions cancel-

Blot-blank-each other out.
Claim-counter claim.
Total exposure.
Eclipse.
Back-to square one.

Some say she's a 'fake', a 'Charlatan'.
Not a mystic!
A woman of esoteric, eclectic and holistic interests-perhaps-
But a cynical, complete and total fraud.
A faker-not a fakir.
But-I notice-that they always shy away from
All of the inexplicable, supernatural,
Phenomena attributed to her.

Others say that she's, 'for real'
And has authentic, great-perhaps actually-unique powers.
Some say she has the power
To induce permanent catatonia,
In a subject-instantly-just by her 'thought power'.
Others say-she can relieve it-
By the same method-within seconds-
In those subjects,
That already have it.

Some say she is 'chaste'-
Too 'spiritually evolved'-
To require physical or sexual love.
Her natural passions, sublimated,
Into her 'great, selfless healing,
Contacting, locating and rescuing work',
For the benefit of all humankind.

Others say-
That she delights
In ecstatic, diabolical, joyous sexual orgies.
Surrounded by a chanting chorus-
A circle of naked, 'fellow devil worshipers'.
That she has sexual intercourse-
With up to a dozen male partners.
She herself being the 'high priestess'-
Her fellow sister priestess's,
Joining in the 'action',
Only after the fortune teller is under way.
The men are treated with great contempt,
It is part of the 'ritual'-
And are verbally abused, degraded, ridiculed,

Mocked and whipped-
With very small-but stinging whips!
Once back on her feet,
She shouts and raves abuse
At the men in fluent German-
While whipping them all mercilessly-
They claim she is a real, genuine sadist.
Often-loudly singing old German war songs,
As she joyously flogs them-laughing-
"Grovel! You pansy liberals! Grovel! Grovel!
That's all you're good for!"
She lashes them and kicks them merrily.
While, they 'worship' the other women.

High on the wall,
Some witnesses have revealed-
Is a huge old painting-
Of her oldest known, ancestor.
A Prussian-a Teutonic Knight-
From the 14th century.
Much decorated.
Hans von Keller. Sword at his side,
In full, shining armour.
A very tall, large, blonde, blue eyed,
Formidable, coldly fierce-looking warrior,
Surveying the scene-
Beneath him,
With an icy disdain.

When the 'orgy' is concluded,
And after refreshments-
(Orgies-after all-are thirsty work),
The satanic ceremony begins.
A living sacrifice-sometimes animal-
More often a human-
Is offered up in blasphemous rites,
On an improvised altar to, 'Satan'.
Satan is represented by an image-
Or a painted statue.
Sometimes by an actor,
In elaborate costume.
Some say the devil himself,
Now and then shows up,
In person and socializes.

The prince of darkness-
If and when he does turn up-

Nicholas Alexander Papantoniou

Always unannounced-
Is very informal-but not very chatty-
Very laid back-wearing dark glasses.
Exhorts them to evil deeds-
And then goes.

Furthermore, eyewitnesses,
Whom I have personally spoken to
Insist-that there was normally
Also a, 'big dragon', or a, 'huge monster',
Attending these orgies and rites.
A dragon-about nine or ten feet tall-
With huge talons,
Massive, folded wings,
A grey-green and scaly hide,
A long spiked tail and slanting yellow eyes.
The dragon is reported to,
'Flap its huge wings in approval',
Causing, rather a perceptible draft-
And has been heard,
'Roaring ', every now and then-
At the proceedings.
The witnesses said, they believed,
That the 'dragon' was a kind of a, 'bouncer',
Or a 'doorman', or guard,
Keeping people out,
Or keeping people in,
At these gatherings.
I simply report. But it is worth mentioning, that
Not one of the three eyewitnesses at these orgies-
That I had tested-two men and one woman-
Was either inebriated or
'High' on drugs-at the time-
Furthermore-I insisted-
They each take a polygraph test-
Which they duly passed,
Each and every one of them.

The ceremonial victim,
Or sacrifice, incidentally,
If human-is usually a, 'hobo'-
Always male, a vagrant, drug-addict,
Homeless person-someone whom,
No one would soon, easily or readily miss.
Often a hapless, illegal immigrant,
'Undocumented'-a Mexican-referred to
During the ritual to as a 'wet back', or the 'spic',

Fresh across the border-
Is chosen-since they are ideal for the purpose-
And there is an abundant supply.
Victims are 'procured',
(Kidnapped), by a trusted follower-himself a Mexican-
Rumoured to be a very busy human trafficker-
Or smuggler-of illegal immigrants-
An entrepreneur of flesh-
Who is reliable and extremely
Well paid for his services.
The ceremony ends-
With a human sacrifice-
Now ready for dissection-
Carried high-bodily to Lucifer.

The orgies and rites always
Take place in a 'safe' house-
Never at her own house.
But a place, secret-always different-heavily guarded,
And equipped with both high-tech
Surveillance and sound-proof rooms.

Of course, her defenders say this rumour is all-
Childish, crazy, spooky stuff-ridiculous-trash.
'B' movie nonsense-with some very grotesque, kinky,
Pornography thrown in.
And-anyone-would have to be really stupid-to believe it!

Now, I simply repeat the stories I have heard.
And I do apologize, for any distress it may have caused
To those-and I know there are many-
Who are of a, 'sensitive nature,'
Or to any devout or followers, of, 'political correctness',
But it was unavoidable.
I cannot tell my tale-without telling the truth.
The whole truth.
No matter how unpalatable it may sometimes be.
And I am determined to tell it.

But -you know-they do have a point-her defenders-
It does sound totally loopy!
Human sacrifice. Initiations. Dancing skeletons in closets.
Nazi gold. Secret rooms. Monsters. Diabolic rites.
Floggings. Magical spells!
It's really too absurd!
It would be extremely comical-under different circumstances.
I thought so myself, at first.

Nicholas Alexander Papantoniou

I do so enjoy a good laugh.
I laughed aloud when I heard about the, 'Aryan or white vow',
The 'Nazi gold,' and so forth.
But some of the testimony-
Which I haven't shared,
(It's much too graphic and violent
And disturbing for retelling, here.)
Is oddly, detailed and convincing.
It troubles me.
I've stopped chortling.

However-this version-was-
It has been conjectured, by some of the F.T.'s protector's-
Also 'put out', by this same anonymous, mysterious,
'Rival' psychic, ten years back-in order to ruin
Her paranormal business-by declaring her to be-both
A neo-Nazi and a Satanist combined-two things-
Most dreadfully alarming-
To ultra-liberal sensibilities-particularly the former.
She would presumably loose all her,
Jewish, black, Asian, Arab, Latino, homosexual
And even her Christian clientele-
Not leaving her with very much left!
A Machiavellian plan-if only so.

But of course-
If that was the plan-it didn't work.
Her business is absolutely booming.
There's sometimes a long, long wait-
Just to get a consultation.
So no one-it seems-
Believed the stories.
Or took them seriously.
She herself-often openly laughs
And jokes about them.

Devil worship? Nazi stuff?
Personally, it does all strike me
As a little too mad, colourful, kinky,
And melodramatic, to be believed.
Although-of course-
It could-
All be true.

So perhaps you ask-
Well, why not charge her with
These dark, dreadful crimes?

Well, how?
And precisely, what crimes-by the way?
There is, after all-no proof,
There are no known victims,
No forensic evidence.
No physical evidence-no material evidence-
Just hearsay. Just rumour.
Everything, is cleaned up, afterwards.
No body or bodies. No witness or witnesses.
Nothing. All-as usual-is opaque.
No one-who would dare-or be 'allowed',
To give evidence or testimony.
And is my belief that any-person or persons-
Building a case against our-little tarot card user-
Would meet with-well-some accidents!
Finally, no one is really certain whether any-
Or all of these allegations-or 'crimes',
Are even true, or half true, or part true-or utterly false.
Let alone provable. I'm not even sure! I'm far from sure!
Perhaps, the suicide journalist-was lying through his teeth-
In order to come up with a sensational story.
Perhaps, he was having a mental breakdown.
Perhaps, he was the victim of an elaborate practical joke.
Perhaps, the fortune woman was, 'playing', him-all along.
And perhaps-even if not-they were all 'fakes'-faking it-
Role-playing, between sadomasochistic, kinky, but
Consenting adults-into bondage and Nazi memorabilia,
Even the Mexicans, the monsters, and what have you.
It does happen,
Whatever you may think of it.
I personally don't approve-
But then I'm just a little old fashioned on these matters.
I don't even like the casual proliferation of pornography
In our society. But I grew up-after all-in a different generation-
I accept that many do-and shrug.
Anyway-these alleged orgies-perhaps-
It was all just very kinky but harmless-fun.

And there are stories that she is 'protected'
By powers, 'very high up',
In the government-it's rumoured-
On account of her extreme 'usefulness'.
This I don't believe.
But-it's not impossible.

It is also rumoured
That she uses her incredible

'Mind-searching powers'-
To root out secrets and-
To blackmail anyone too, 'curious', about her.
And I do mean anyone!
I have heard some very,
Very big names thrown around.
But add it all up-and-you'll see-
There is a very large hole-
In this particular donut!

There is also a story of two parties-
And I can give their first names,
As 'Sally' and her partner' Joel',
Who-let us say-had some sort
Of material conflict with,
Our dear-local crystal ball gazer.
It is alleged that after-either a séance-
Or a hypnosis-she trapped, removed-and held-
Their souls or ectoplasms-
In a state of, 'Suspension'
For several hours-or several days-
According to which anecdote you care to follow-
And that she, 'levitated and span' their ectoplasms-
Both now in violent convulsions and spasms-
Around her living room-and all around her flower garden-
Like two 'flying frisbees '.
Until the two persons, 'came to their senses'-
And she returned them to their bodies.
Both were apparently a good deal terrified
And chastened by the ordeal.
Sally soon moved to Las Vegas
And has since become a drug addict.
Joel-it seems-never recovered,
From his experience,
Suffered a nervous breakdown-
And is now in an institution.

So if you see a discarnate spirit-
Or a disembodied soul-
One named Sally-the other named Joel-
Floating by your house-one afternoon.
Why-don't be alarmed-don't worry-
No need for dismay!

Though for some this might seem
To be a real panic-bringer-
Or a true fear-sweller,

It is just another dull, boring, working day,
For the fortune teller.

I have also heard,
A curious account-rather recently-
From a ex-neighbour of the mesmerist.
An affluent-otherwise very honest-retired woman,
Now in her sixties.

She claims that she witnessed
One hot summers day-about ten years ago-
Watching from her own garden fence -
Only 25 feet away-while having an ice-cold drink-
An argument between,
The fortune teller and some ,'rival', psychic.
The woman swears that the fortune teller
Caused this young man to-
'Melt '. Yes.
That's right-
Melt.

They were having this heated argument.
The fortune teller accused the rival psychic-
Of telling people terrible, 'lies', about her.
Telling people that she was a Nazi-
That she was a Satanist-
That she was a witch.
That she was a murderess.
That she was a nymphomaniac.
That she practiced all kinds of dark magic.
That she could fly.
He denied it vehemently.
She insisted that she had proof!
Then there was a pause.
Apparently, the fortune teller said,
Looking up at the blue sky, in a casual way:
'Isn't it warm today?'
Gestured, with her hands,
Whereupon her rival-
I quote from the said, neighbour:

"...Suddenly swayed and cried out in surprise-
And then screamed out in utter horror:
'Not that! No! Please! Please! God!
Not that! Brigit-for the love of God-not that!'
And he started to sink and shrink and soften,
Swaying sideways and began slowly melting,

Like an ice-cream cone, left out,
In the sun-too long, on a hot, summers day.
His features disappeared. Melted. Blurred.
Lost all their clarity and definition.
But-it wasn't like he was burning or anything-
No! There was absolutely no heat at all!
It was more like he was just turning into mush.
The guy was just getting smaller and wobblier
And sort of bendy and droopy and curvy and curly-
And he was rolling, slanting, sagging,
Listing, side to side.
Like a jelly-or custard-or a mousse-
And collapsing and wiggling-rippling-layering-
Undulating like a wave-as an invertebrate-
Like a man of clay-on a potter's wheel.
A boneless thing.
He was just-like-folding-rolling-and dripping away!
I could hardly believe my own eyes!
And his voice was getting higher
And thinner and funnier.
He was screaming, shrieking, protesting.
Beseeching, imploring-begging her to stop,
In a strange, funny,
High, squeaky, little, falsetto voice!
'...No Brigit! Stop! Stop! Brigit! Please! Please! Please!
Stop! I beg you...!'
From a living human being-
He was turning into a frothy,
Cascading, flowing, pudding-like ooze.
 A mushy-man. A wobbly-gobbly, bubbly goo!
Spilling over. Bubbling. Splashing.
He was just dissolving-liquefying-
Holes and gaps and vacancies and spaces
Were forming and opening in his body-
Right before my very eyes!
Till he was like a fluid, creamy,
Strawberry, growing, pouring pool,
Of a human milkshake!
Soon, all that was left of him, was a big, pink, foaming,
Puddle on the grass-still evaporating
And-fizzing a little-even as I watched him-
In amazement and horror and pity.
Just like a pink whipped cream man.
Man-pulp!
I swear, it only took about a minute.
Afterwards, the fortune teller calmly
Walked over-

Looked across the garden,
Down at the results of her work.
Looked satisfied.
Nodded and grunted.
Then looked directly at me.
Winked at me,
Put her forefinger,
To her lips!
As though to say;
'Shhh. Don't-tell anybody!
Our little secret!'
(It seemed like a very significant warning to me.)
She then coolly went
And scraped him up off the lawn, with a spade,
Into an old, rusty tin can and tossed him,
Carelessly into the trash!
She picked up his clothes-with a slight smile-
And she said in her heavy German accent;
"Oh! Look, at this, now! Look! Look! Really!
I ask you! Some people must always leave,
Such a dreadful mess behind them!
So inconsiderate! You always have to
Clean up after them! So selfish!
Spilling, dripping, splashing, spurting,
Squirting all over the fence and everywhere!
What a sloppy man! Not the slightest bit
Of common consideration for the other person!
That's the problem with our society! No manners anymore!
Some people-they never once have the simple courtesy-
To think of the mess their making!"
She tut-tut-tut-ed crossly.
Then she put the man's clothes in the garbage,
And smiled at me warmly and said it was
'Such a lovely day', and went into her house.
She seemed to be in a very good mood.
I was shaking with fear as she passed by me!
My teeth were chattering-and like I said-
It was a hot and beautiful day.
I was too terrified to think clearly,
About this for a long time.
I told no one.
And who on earth would ever believe me anyway?
I couldn't believe it!
I told myself, again and again-I imagined it-all of it-but-oh-
But I know what I saw and heard
And witnessed that day!
It was so horrible and so ugh! I can't describe it!

So I never told anyone-
Until you..."

Soon after this incident occurred-
The woman relocated to Oregon.
I haven't heard from her since.
But she swears-
Swears on the life of her five children-
That she saw it all happen-
One quiet, high summer afternoon,
Ten years ago.

Now it's quite unequivocally mad of course.
It's unmitigated, banana puree.
It's a nice slice, of old, nutty, fruitcake.
It's deplorably deranged.
It's utter, freaking lunacy!
I report it as I do all else-
Impartially.
But-well-one simply shakes ones head.
I do-at least!

I can say-about the source of the story
Of the apparently,
Remarkable, emollient power
Of the fortune teller-
Without revealing her identity;
Although now, 'clean'-
Back in the sixties and seventies,
As a 'hippie', and very young-
She 'experimented' for years
With many different 'substances'.
Perhaps-one might say more accurately-
The substances, 'experimented' with her.
The whole LSD, psychedelic-trip or bit or thing
Or bag, drag or hang up or addiction.
And this is the final result.
One more delayed casualty
Of the counter-culture, drugs,
The permissive society-
And the Woodstock generation.
Far-out, groovy days!
Now, back to real life.

Another person claims,
That the fortune teller-
Has a secret fortune!

A war-chest, worth untold millions,
Of gold ingots, weighing, 'tons',
'Stashed', away somewhere in New England.
The source-now retired-formerly employed
In Israel's intelligence services, Mossad-
Had discovered a trail leading to her-
When searching for Nazi war criminals.
He claims it is Nazi gold and treasure-
Plundered, from all over Europe, during the war.
Was smuggled by her S.S. Totenkopf-relatives,
Out of Berlin, In the final days-
When the Reich-faced certain defeat.
The loot was then taken by ship.
Guarded by a brave, loyal and trusted junior S.S. officer-
Described by one undisclosed
Source, as a 'blond giant',
A man of enormous physical strength-
Perhaps, to help in carrying the gold-
And disguised as a Swedish sailor.
The ship-with its gold hidden under crates of tinned food-
Sailed from Spain or Portugal-others say from Sweden or Denmark,
To Brazil or Argentina or Peru or Chile
Or Paraguay or Bolivia or Uruguay-
The 'source', really isn't sure-
But where the tellers relatives,
Had Nazi contacts-already in situ.
Half of it was 'moved',
To the fortune-makers residence-
Thirty two years after the end of the war-
That would be in 1977.
The other half stayed with the hiding,
Nazi expatriates-so they could, 'live it up', a little.
The source claims that the total could be as
High as 250,000,000 dollars in gold-judging
The price of gold, by the ounce, in the current market.
Other sources say that this is just,
Fiddlesticks. Poppycock. Balderdash.
There was no gold. No treasure.
No Nazi loot. No S.S. smugglers.
More 'B' movie, claptrap!
More lies, to blacken the name of the fortune teller,
A totally spiritual woman, with a great gift
For healing, finding, contacting the beyond.
More lies-all promulgated by doctrinaire
Atheists, agnostics, secularists, scientists,
Who worry profoundly-
That she is providing real,

Nicholas Alexander Papantoniou

Living 'proof',
Of the after-life.

Her defenders state,
That far from having, 'millions, in gold bars',
The fortune teller lives and always has
Lived-rather frugally-is not very materialistic-
For example-she only has one house and one car-
And as has been stated before-
Gives a lot of money to many
And diverse charities.
(Jewish and Latin American among them.)
This is provable fact. Not silly rumour or innuendo or gossip.
But earns a lot herself-from her psychic works-
And pays all her taxes-
Like a good American citizen!

But-you know,
Question.
If she really had all the powers attributed to her-
Why would she even need gold?
Answer?
She wouldn't.

Finding the truth of the fortune teller,
Is like moving in a maze-
There is nothing clear or sharp at all-
Everything is haze!
But you always-somehow-always-
Feel her watching gaze-
Following you-
As you search.

So if you think-all this-
Is just plain crazy, loony or sick-
Then-run, just run my friend-
Run-pretty quick-
There'll be another hex or spell-real soon-
If you miss one-
Don't wait for her to flick,
You into another dimension-
With just her little finger-
And don't try to mix-or try any tricks-
You dumb hicks-with super psychics-
Such as this one.
You'll only loose-
Like all the others.

It is hard-very hard-
To know what's true
About our diabolic dame-
Or innocent mystic.
Some say that she even
Has a daughter-Trudi-
From an unknown and discarded husband,
Right now-being raised and educated in Germany-
In a small village in Bavaria.

Some say she has 'caused'
More than a dozen, brutal murders.
Others say she has-in fact-
At great personal risk-
'Prevented' them.
Some say she has caused many scores-
If not hundreds-of fatal 'accidents',
Others say she has 'halted' them.
Some say that through
'Auto-suggestion', she can
Make, 'demons or ghouls or monsters', appear.
Others say that she can rid
And 'cleanse' the subjects mind,
Of such hallucinations,
By her intense 'thought power'.

Some say that she has reduced, 'dozens',
Of her 'enemies', to a vegetative state-
Simply by the nameless and unknowable horrors,
Which she unleashed on them-
All of them-
Now committed to padded cells.

It is said that she can 'remote read' minds
From almost any distance-
If she goes into a trance-like state.
Regular mind reading is,
'A piece of cake', for her.
It is believed that she first
Discovered these abilities
When she was as young
As four or five.

Her world-
Whatever the truth of it-which-
May eventually be proven in God's clear

Daylight-is so full of-shadows.
Deep, dark, ominous, pervasive-shadows!
And I don't know if she is a saint or a sinner.
A perpetrator of monstrous and prolific crimes,
Or-a victim of awful and diabolical lies.
Is there an evil design-back of it all?
Or simply an arbitrary confluence,
Of random and unrelated events?
All-versions-all partake of the same-
Constantly forming and re-forming-
Woven and inter-woven-amorphous-
Dark and unsubstantial and maddening-shadows.
You just can't see or judge anything clearly.

But we have-
After all-free will.
I am no determinist.
No follower of moral relativity.
No ethical revisionist.
Free choice.
We have all bitten of the tree,
Of the knowledge of good and evil
And we know its flavour-
The taste of each.
Whether we deceive ourselves or no-
Admit it or deny it or not.
All of us. We know.
The demon tempter,
Who beckons us-all our life-to sin.
Or the guardian angel,
Who calls us-all of our lives-to virtue.
We follow at their behest.
Perhaps, yes. But we follow!
Our choice.
No one else's.
We must all of us take-
Finally-take-responsibility
For our actions.
The fortune teller-
She also knows.

I-personally-
Am not a superstitious person.
Never have been.
I am a rationalist-an empiricist.
An optimist-to a degree-but a realist.
Most people find me an eminently

Sane, calm and logical fellow.
But-of course-we all have moments
When were not!
I say this so that you neither assume
That I'm a total sceptic-a philistine-
If you will-on these matters,
But nor am I a kind of, 'fidei defensor',
Of the paranormal and supernatural.
An academic and historian-since
I left the state department.
A 'show me'- kind of guy-
Though-actually-I'm not
From the great state of Missouri-
I was born and raised here, in Georgetown.
Call me a doubting Thomas.
My first thought-
When I began to get interested in her-
Was that it was all absolute hogwash!
I was positively amused that anyone
Could possibly believe such stuff and nonsense!
It was all so primitive and superstitious.
Such antediluvian attitudes abounded!
Such atavistic impulses seemed to beckon one!
But I have begun-in recent years-to think again.
There are rather too many strange, spooky stories,
Weird, harrowing tales, uncanny happenings,
Accidents, fatalities, coincidences,
Lurid deaths and mad,
Nutty narratives concerning-our very own,
Brigit Astrid Keller.
Perhaps now-
Just perhaps-
I'm starting to be-a believer.

We live
Our lives,
Adorned with beauty,
Battered by the admonitions
And depredations of time and circumstance.
We look for the light.
The darkness isn't real-you see-
It is only the absence of light.
But equally-and paradoxically-
Darkness becomes real-in the absence of light.
If you wish to understand our universe-
Philosophically-anyway-
You will have to understand the relationship

Between the light and the dark.
And sometimes that's not easy-
Not easy at all-that is what I have learned,
From following in the wake of the fortune arbiter.
Herself-so full of light and so full of darkness.
And so difficult it is-to tell-which is which.
For it all seems so-utterly and inextricably blended.
Things can be far weirder,
Than they ever seem on a calm, cool day.
If I've learned nothing else-from her-
I have learned, that-
And it's something
I won't forget.

Positive. Negative.
Light, dark. Good, evil.
Rough. Smooth. Good witch. Bad witch.
You can't ditch the witch!
But which witch-is the real one?
And what if a good witch will-switch-
With a bad witch-
The better to conceal one?

The fortune teller-sees all,
Sees-far more than is apparent,
She looks deep into your soul,
Her giant eyes-transparent.

Sceptic, rationalist, empiricist,
Who's spiritual faculties are blunted.
Come, meet the fortune teller!
Thus-the hunter becomes-the hunted.

The fortune teller-well-she tells your fortune!
Will you live long-when will you die?
She knows-for a fact-when you tell the truth,
She knows-for certain-when you lie.

The fortune teller, knows the murderer, the serial-killer,
The rapist, the fraud, the false and the true.
You cannot hide from her haunting gaze-
No matter what you do!

That such things are-and such things are not,
The disbeliever can assume,
But no one can comprehend anything at all,
Within a spiritual vacuum.

The thesis, is the life of spirit,
The antithesis, is the life of matter,
The synthesis-is the spiritual seer,
Despite-all dialectic data.

Many can-and do-argue the facts,
And analyze the symptoms in various ways,
But no one can interpret, unseen acts,
On dianoetic days!

What does the fortune teller mean to you?
What does she mean to me?
A palpitating paradox,
A weird dichotomy!

She can spot a casual duplicity.
Catch a lie, without hesitation.
It is whispered that she has assisted in recent,
Hard-core, terrorist interrogations.

Her knowledge-her vision-it is said-
Shines a torch-illuminates a path.
Her accuracy is 'reckoned' to be,
Superior-to a polygraph.

Without going into details-which I can't do-
What exactly can I-truthfully-say?
She has worked happily, with F.B.I.
She has worked harmoniously, with the C.I.A.

Highly ranked officials,
Have said of her results,' She's the tops',
In counter-espionage, anti-terrorist, 'assistance',
In 'surveillance', and 'black ops'.

Time after time, she has helped,
Break-up organized crime-and revealed-
'Undercover' spies, multiple rapists, fugitives,
Child-killers, drug traffickers-all deeply concealed.

So if they want to find a major serial killer,
Or interview a, 'visitor' interstellar,
Please, go see-a New England psychic-
They call-the fortune teller.

It is rumoured that she has known,

What no one else-or very few-
Have ever known or seen,
It is said that she has, 'psychically probed,'
A captured, genuine-'alien' being.

In the end she does what she wants to-
No one can make or force her.
Whether it be, finding a helpless kidnap victim.
Or interviewing the occupant-of a flying saucer.

Thus her little
'Transgressions', 'eccentricities',
'Hobbies', 'pastimes', 'social evenings',
Are happily overlooked.
All forgotten, forgiven-it is said-
All the clients who are
Now stark raving mad-
The others who wound up dead.

Thus she leads a life-
So quiet, serene, tranquil and surreptitious,
And it holds-perhaps-many secrets-
Horrible, terrible, dreadful and vicious.

The details of her life are so malleable,
But to her new country-
She is far-far-too valuable-
To ever be lost.

And most of all-considering all the evil-
Most of all I ask this:
Is she the point of origin?
Or just-the catalyst?

So, you see,
It is not just her lucky charms-
A four-leaf clover-
A rabbit foot-
Or Coffee dregs-
Or her tarot cards she uses,
Still it is always her enemies,
Always her rivals,
And-always you-
That loses.

This is not a jest,
Heed my warning-lest-

You meet an actual,
Genuine, modern-
Sorceress.

So, now boys and girls!
If you want to play-
Yes! If you are an occult player,
You can peel layer,
After layer after layer,
Away from this soothsayer
And never learn the truth!
Play nice!

And thus,
The fortune teller-dwells in darkness,
And the fortune teller-lives in light.
And no one ever truly sees her,
With clear, unblemished sight.

And whether her 'magic' is black,
Or whether her' magic' is white,
And is it human suffering-or human joy-
That gives her such intense delight?

And no one knows for sure,
Who is wrong and who is right.
And whether she blossoms in brightest day,
Or dooms-in the darkest night!

And whether-she truly can bless,
Or whether-she really can blight.
And whether-she plunders
The deeps of the soul,
Or whether-she scales the height.

And why she gives some,
Such a very warm feeling,
And others-such a terrible fright.

And whether she uses
Her powers-good or evil-
With all her awesome might!

And in the eternal battle
Between good and evil-
On which side does she fight?

And whether it is just superstition-
Waxed rampant?
Well, no. I think. Not quite!

Does she abide-
In the attic of the soul,
Or does she inhabit the cellar?
But-who really knows-
Anything for sure-
About our fortune teller?

Does she give sweet,
Angelic gifts and boons?
With plangent and graceful tunes-
Or is she an evil-speller?
The one man who could tell the tale-
Never ever, ever told -
Of the fortune teller!

Now comes,
The final stretch of our odd, little odyssey,
The apotheosis of weirdness and mystery,
Following, forever following-in the temporal slipstream,
Of a blonde who has far too much fun.
And I have sometimes,
Made my way-as before-
Surrounded by shadows-
Almost, as a blind man, struggling, labouring,
Fumbling-in the dark.

Her grandfather-
Heinz Keller-
During the second world war-
Was a German rocket scientist,
Helping to create
The 'wonder weapons', technology,
Beyond even the V2-
Such as flying saucers, jet planes,
The famous, 'fly trap' and so forth.

At the end of the war,
He was brought to America,
With around two hundred other elite German,
Rocket scientists, to help the U.S. with its
Own missile program and also make sure
The Russians didn't get them first.
The cold war-

Before world war two-was quite over
Even then-was taking a definite shape.
This transfer of scientists, of course,
Was called project ,'Paperclip'.

Now-I must condense-
In the interest of brevity.
There are those who say that
The fortune teller's entire power,
Derives, from an encounter with an
Injured-in fact-dying, crash-landed-
Alien.

Some say, it was at Roswell.
Others say it was at some other-unknown location.
The story goes like this.

Heinz Otto Keller-apparently, by sheer luck-
Was the first man to be at the scene
Of the 'crash landed', flying saucer.
He was on a long evening drive home.

He had seen something, 'glowing',
Falling from the sky-
Heard an explosion, less than a mile away.
It was after sunset-but not quite dark.
By pure chance his daughter-
Hilda-then seventeen-was with him-
They-naturally-drove to the scene-
To see if they could help,
Thinking it was a small, private airplane.
Stopped the car-got out-to see what had crashed.
To their amazement, it appeared to be
A UFO and a badly injured alien-lying on the earth-
A few yards from the debris.
While Heinz, rushed back to his car
To get his Kodak colour camera-and put film in it-
Hilda-a soulful girl-rushed to the dying alien's side
And tried to comfort it.
(The alien is believed to have been male,
Though the differences between the sexes
Of this race appear to have been negligible.)
Hilda offered the expiring alien-a candy bar, coca cola, water,
A chicken sandwich and a peanut butter and jelly
Sandwich by turns.
The alien perhaps could not eat human food-
Or perhaps was too badly injured to do so.

It did-sip some cold water,
And a little coca-cola-without apparent ill effects.
The alien was lying on the ground-by the crashed UFO.
He was described as, 'small, thin and green with
A disproportionately huge head and big, dark, oval eyes.'
He-or it-was bleeding a very dark green blood.
Hilda spoke to him, stroked his head gently, held his hand,
And put a sweater under his head-as a pillow-and tried
To communicate with the creature,
And offered gentle words of commiseration and sympathy.
Even sang a song-or a lullaby-to make the alien feel a little better.

It is believed that this alien-
As all of its race-was possessed
Of super-intelligence, far beyond even
The most brilliant human mind.
It is conjectured-that the alien was strangely touched-
By this strange tenderness and kindness-
So far from home-from one alien life form to another.
The girl was quite without hate, fear, doubt, anger or suspicion-
And just wanted to help.

It is hypothesized that,
He placed his small yellow-green hands on the teenagers
Blonde head-while cupping her forehead tightly.
She felt an- '...incredible flow of energy,
A blinding flash of white light,
In the centre of my forehead and right behind my eyes.'
This was almost the alien's last act.
It said something softly to the girl-but of course-
She could not understand the words.
It is believed that it was an expression
Of thanks or gratitude for her kindness.

It is believed that the alien,
With almost its last breath-
Then gave the girl a small, translucent blue disk-
About-an inch and a quarter-in diameter.

Having put the disc in the girls hand,
The alien immediately, slumped over and died.
Hilda wept, kissed the aliens forehead.
She was an intensely religious girl-
Then said a brief, heartfelt prayer for the departed alien's soul.
She put the disc in her pocket, wiped her tears,
And thought no more of it.
Her grandfather-a tall, thin, fair-haired, energetic, wiry man-

Returned with his camera and swore and stamped his foot,
When he realized that The ET was dead.
But he took a lot of colour pictures
Of the creature-from all angles-and of the crashed UFO.
Exclaiming, laughing and cackling;
"Mein Gott! Unglaubiche! Gott in Himmel! Nicht-in mein lieben!
Der ganze welt! The whole world will be so astonished!
"This will make us famous! Hilda-baby-ya! Wunderbar!
Wunderbar! Welch ein tag! This will make us rich! Rich!"
He took pictures-while Hilda was still crying and sobbing.
It was then that the military turned up.

The alien was quickly taken away to be, 'examined'.
The crashed saucer was also confiscated, quickly taken away,
In several trucks to be, 'studied.'
Heinz Keller's camera and film was confiscated,
"It's all government property now, pal!"
He was told, by a tall, burly sergeant,
When he vigorously protested.
"Buddy-you may be a hot-shot, kraut scientist-
But I got my orders! You know how it goes. Orders are orders.
Right? Yeah, sure-sure you do."
And he and Hilda were both sworn to utter secrecy.
Then they were both quickly taken away in a jeep-
And relentlessly interrogated for days-
By dozens of 'scientists', at a secret location.
They did not-of course-know anything about the disc.
Somehow, they did not think
To search the girl's, pockets.

It is said that they both later met President Truman-
And later President Eisenhower,
Vice-and future-President Nixon and later-
President John F. Kennedy and vice-
And future-President Johnson.
They also met John Glenn and Robert McNamara,
And were asked and answered many questions-
About their encounter.
They were each given, signed autographs,
And a, 'top-secret', presidential medal.
Her grandfather-who of course-was then working for NASA-
Also got promoted and a very generous raise in pay-
For his, 'nice, quick-thinking, go-getting,
On the ball, can-do, right-stuff, all-American initiative.'
And they already knew that he was good-
Very good-
At keeping secrets.

It is conjectured that the alien-
In 'touching' Hilda's head,
Transferred all his 'powers', to her.
The disc-it is hypothesized-
 Enables the owner to 'store'
And 'renew', and 're-charge',
All these transferred, 'alien', powers.
And tap into their alien,
Racial memories and vast expanse and vistas of
Experience, knowledge and-also their language.

Hilda Keller-was the teenage girl-
Who was given the blue object.
She, gave birth to a daughter-
Brigit-eleven years later.

She gave her daughter the disc-
As a toy-when the girl was five.
And told her always to keep it safe
And never to give it or show it to anyone.
It was, 'very precious, beautiful and rare.'
The disc remained unknown to anyone,
Except mother and daughter.
Who were extremely close.
The girl often played with it.

Hilda did not tell her father-Heinz Keller-
About the disc-since she knew he would
Take it from her.
So the fortune tellers,
Grandfather was never,
Aware of its existence.

Brigit's mother-Hilda-incidentally-
Was a beautiful girl.
There is a striking family resemblance.
Both blonde. Tall. Slim. Graceful. Elegant.
Same fine, clean cut, 'Aryan', features.
I have seen pictures of her taken when she was seventeen.
She was a girl-by all accounts-with a remarkably
Kind, sweet, gentle and compassionate disposition.
She was always rescuing and trying to help stray dogs,
And cats, snakes, lame horses and injured birds.
And perhaps-just perhaps-
One other-far more
Distant, lost, stray and injured creature.

It is said the fortune teller has
Stayed in 'contact' with
The ancient, alien civilization,
Across unimaginable
Distances of time and space,
Through, 'remote' telepathy.

Brigit-inherited all her mother's,
Alien-given powers.
Her mother rarely ever used them-
And then only modestly
And discreetly.

Although her daughter-and only child-
Brigit-was cut from a different cloth.
She had more of the ambitious, bold,
Rather arrogant, character
Of her Prussian grandparents-
Heinz and Anna-
Both of whom-by the way-
Lived very happily, very peacefully-
And very contentedly-
In Wisconsin,
Well into their nineties.

Of Brigit's father-
Horst-little is known.
He was from the Rhineland.
Although some sources say
He was from Bavaria.
He left her mother
To return to Germany,
When Brigit was just a baby.
She never knew him at all.
It is a bit of a mystery.
All I know of him is that he was
A confirmed pacifist and, 'a very nice man.'

At any rate-
This disk restores all her 'powers'
And indeed increases,
Or magnifies them all-
For both good and ill.
In a nutshell, that's it.

Now, how did I learn all this?

I cannot possibly tell you how.
You would hardly believe it-if I did.
But do I believe it?
No!
I've checked all the checkable details
Of this hypothesis-years ago-interviewed dozens-
Under conditions, of the greatest, possible secrecy
And confidentiality. Looked at records.
Studied the written accounts. Classified documents.
I find it very unconvincing.
Too many glaring inconsistencies.
Too many holes, flaws. Perforations.
Doesn't hold water.
Although, certain peripheral details-
Such as specifics of time and place-may well be true.
But in essence-no.

In fact, I have very good reason to believe this entire,
'Alien' story', is just pure disinformation-a deliberate, cynical,
Fabrication disseminated-by sources possibly high in the
Government-in order to deflect attention away from the truth
Of Roswell-whatever it may be-sinister or mundane.
And to further obscure the reality of the teller of fortunes-
Including the highly classified, covert and, 'revolutionary',
Work she is now doing, for the government in the realms of
Counter-espionage, national and international security and defence,
As head of the new, and highly classified,
 'Paranormal weapons', department.

I believe, it was all dreamed up
By incorrigible sci-fi devotees,
And nerds and geeks,
Enamoured by the legend-
Or romantic myth,
Of Roswell.

Oh, but yes,
I do believe.
I have become a believer.
A true believer.
Seeing, is believing-I have seen.
I believe-that the powers of the fortune teller-
Whatever they may be,
Are genuine and real
Beyond any truly, 'rational', explanation,
And beyond all doubt-utterly extraordinary.
And natural-and out of this world!

But not given to her by expiring,
And grateful aliens.

And yet-
The 'alien' explanation-
No question-that some absolutely do believe it.

A story is in the telling-
This we all know.
No matter where you are dwelling-
The fortune teller-tells us so.

And having told us,
She moves on.
Up through the shadows-
She is gone-upon-
Her strange, secret, silent way-
To new-and unknown realms!

And so
Must we move on.
Make of all of the above information,
What you will.
If you can make some coherent sense of it,
I doff my hat to you-and bow-metaphorically.
And if you can't make any
Damned sense of it-
Welcome-to my universe!

I only knew one man,
And I knew him very well,
Who once told me that he knew-
The whole truth about our
Little damsel of dire distress,
But he-never, ever told his tale!

Once, we were at Harvard together.
First met him on campus,
Autumn, of 1962.
Ah, yes. I remember. I remember,
It so very vividly, wonderful days!
Everybody was doing the, 'twist'.
I do remember-one mellow afternoon,
Hearing, 'Telstar,' playing distantly, on a radio-
As we both had a hot dog,
And an ice-cold bottle of coca-cola,
And talked politics.

We disagreed about practically everything!
We were both born the same year-1940-
(He June 14-I on December 15) -
That was our one real affinity.
In all other things-we differed.
He liberal-I conservative.
He 'hip'-I- 'square'.
He-short, (five-seven), stocky,
Gregarious and sociable,
I-very tall, (six-five), and very thin,
Studious and reserved.
He dark haired-I blond.
He-an atheist-of the scoffer variety.
I-a Christian-of the protestant persuasion.
But both of us, young, eager,
And passionately patriotic.
Excited by the space race, the new frontier,
The cold war, our young president-
And the amazing zeitgeist,
Of those glorious days.
The sweet and beautiful
And all too tragically,
Brief days-of Camelot.

We were total, utter opposites.
But-despite this-or really because of it-
We became very firm, lasting friends.
Now this-when we met-I should judge-would have been-
About a week-before the Cuban missile crises.
Anyway-it was this man-who said he knew
The 'whole truth' about her.
But never told it.

So he met her-
Many years later-
Our noble or ignoble heroine-was a client.
(He was always inclined to be a tad rash,
And I frequently chided him for it.)

His mind was read.
His palm was read.
His cards were done.
His soul was probed and prodded.
His spirit was searched.
Went to a séance.
Went to an, 'essence cleansing'.
Had a private, 'consultation', with her.

She told him to-
Beware of, 'Relletenutrofeth'.

That he was now,
Going into very deep and dangerous waters,
I think-never occurred to him.
He was as confirmed a secularist-
As he was a bachelor.
That clandestine trajectory-
That parabola of mystery-
That thing which attracts or alarms-
So very many-about our heroine-
I believe-never crossed his mind-
Until it was too late!

He attended a 'group', mind reading, session.
He attended a group essence cleansing.
He found her-by the way-very lovely, sexy.
Intensely, erotically enticing.
Her face-so very mysterious and beautiful.
Her bosom, so very deep and full.
Her eyes, so very wonderful, big and blue.
Her bottom, so very full and soft.
Her voice-so very husky and Teutonic.
Although, she never encouraged him at all.
Indeed, she treated him quite coldly, briskly.
Was very formal, business-like and distant.
But of course, this only turned him on.

And over the months,
A few years ago,
He investigated her.
Traced back her Prussian aristocrat, lineage.
He learned her, 'secrets'- although-
As it turned out-alas-
Not all.

He told her-the damned fool-
That he was,
A bit of a, 'diabolic dabbler.'
So, it seems-one day-he was invited
To a bit of a Satan-worship do.

One madly hot, mid-summer night,
He was driven to the address blindfolded.
(As all first time guests were.)
They changed into costume

In a large, empty, unknown house.
A house with armed guards and sound proof rooms.
He says, he saw the fortune teller,
Standing there-before him-stark naked-
Just briefly-while she was changing-
Into her own outfit.
Said she was,
'Still an incredibly, breathtakingly, beautiful woman-
Entrancing and very youthful looking-
Tall, proud, slender, long legged.
But with great, big, huge, beautiful, bouncing, swaying pink tits-
And a tremendous, shapely ass!'
She; 'Exuded a raw, sexual magnetism.
But she looked so cool, so inscrutable.'
Of course, I always assumed-
She was just a fake. A talented, convincing
Fake, maybe-yeah-sure-but a fake.
Oh! Little did I know.'
Little indeed.

The strange, ritual began-
And obviously I cannot verify this-I wasn't there-
My old friend had always been a little kinky-
Whereas-I was always inclined to be a smidgen-puritanical.
It was another one of our differences!
But now he was in way over his head.
Taking fright from the blood curdling
Satanic ceremony-
Which he had hitherto, believed,
Would be totally sham and bogus-
Just a flimsy excuse for kinky sex-and of course-
His one great chance to have sexual intercourse
With the lovely fortune teller.
But it turned out to be all too real and all too terrible!
He watched. Said-he saw things which he could,
'Neither believe-comprehend-nor even watch!'
He alleges, he saw a human sacrifice,
Dragged, bound, terrified and screaming to the alter-
'Shrieking in Spanish or Mexican or something.'
Approached by a very tall costumed man,
Wielding a long knife,
While people stood watching and chanting in chorus-
Then he saw Beelzebub-
Standing-ten yards away.

He fled.
Says he was chased by a 'dragon',

Down the street and shrubbery-
For a hundred yards-
Barely escaping-
As he left.

That-at any rate-is his story.
He has since-my old Harvard friend-
And cold war buddy-
Become a virtual recluse.
Seldom goes out.
'Relletenutrofeth', he says-is-
'The fortune teller'-spelt, backwards.

If he was a true sceptic-before-
Perhaps now he's an apostate.
But-he is a believer.
He almost never goes out.
He has all his requirements delivered.
In fact he hardly sees anyone, anymore.
Not even me-perhaps-his oldest living friend.
It's a sad case.
I shake my head over it, frequently.

He suffers-he says-from truly terrible,
Mind-bending nightmares.
In which he claims-he sees the fortune teller-
As a witch-laughing-cackling-
Journeying-on a broomstick-
Her huge, deep bosom showing in a very low cut black dress-
Cracking a whip-pursuing him-furiously-
All through outer space!

He informs me that her 'astral body',
Enters his room, under the door,
While he sleeps and 'laughs aloud ', at him-
As he awakens.

He suffers from intense,
Panic/anxiety attacks-at nights.
It is usually at night that she pays, 'visits.'

He has frequent,
Severe stomach cramps, aches-chronic constipation-
And often endures sudden, prolonged
And malodorous attacks-
Of stupendously, violent flatulence.
This ill-wind -he claims-the fortune teller-

Is deliberately causing him-as punishment.
(I am saying nothing.)

Shaking, trembling hands. Chattering teeth.
Shivering fits. Face twitches. Nervous tics.
Bouts of hyperventilation. Paranoia.
These symptoms.
Macabre, appalling, terrible hallucinations-
Lasting seconds.

He-when younger-did take a lot of drugs.
I-personally, was vehemently anti-drugs.
(Another of our differences.)
I wonder-sometimes-
If it might have affected his brain.

He lives in perpetual dread and-speaks-
Of her, 'awful power', her 'spells', her 'magic'
And her, 'strange, sinister, creatures',
He claims, he is being 'watched' and 'observed'
By ordinary cats and dogs and birds-who report back to her.
Squirrels and spiders and beetles and bugs and ants all-
Following him down the street-on her orders.
Afterwards-he claims-they also report back to her.
He suffers from mad delusions.
He is going off his head.

He asserts that he once saw her,
In flight.
'Flying', or 'floating' or 'gliding',
One evening-outside-his house.
At sunset,
Above his garden-
Slowly-smoothly-effortlessly-hovering-circling around
The house-which is quite hidden behind tall trees.
Looking in through the windows and curtains-
Tapping on them gently.
Waving to him and very softly-
Calling out his name!

He tells me-that one day-he saw,
Her transparent, glowing, 'astral' body,
Walking, 'through', all the walls of his house,
Up through the ceiling and down through
The floors-softly-casually-leisurely-as if they
Were made of nothing-but air.
Her astral body, walked right up to him,

And said in a shimmering, vibrating, pulsing voice-
Which sounded very near, very clear-
But very distant and far away;
"You are a fool! I warned you! You are a weakling!
You should have listened! Now-I curse you!
You shall soon be our sacrifice!
Your days are numbered!"
Then she turned and walked right through
All the walls and was gone.

He swears that-
She sometimes sends a skeleton-
A living, walking, turning, quickly,
Jerkily moving skeleton-to search his house.
The skeleton walks into his room-
Its skull and bones-gleaming in the dark-
Late at night-when he is in bed-
Bathed in moonlight-
From the large bedroom windows.
And-motionless-just gazes at him for a long time.
Then the skeleton, looks around,
Up and down, in the closet and under the bed,
In the cupboards and in the bathroom.
Then-he told me-it starts to dance.
Dancing right in front of him-all around the room.
Sometimes quickly. Sometimes slowly.
Sometimes stopping. Then abruptly starting again.
Staggering. oscillating, shaking, bending, marching.
It dances the Charleston.
It also does the twist.
It dances for one or two minutes-abruptly stops.
Then walks away-gnashing and chattering, its teeth audibly.
It enters and leaves somehow-
By climbing through a window.
He informs me that it can climb very well-
Being all bone-and therefore very light and quiet.
My old friend really believes-
That this actually occurs.
What can I say?
It's so sad.
It's crackpot stuff.

My once energetic, extraverted, confidant friend-
A boon companion,
Has been reduced, to a pitiful, pathetic,
Frightened, hyperventilating valetudinarian!
On the point of a nervous breakdown.

Mumbling about alien-
Visitors sent by her-to remonstrate with him.
I have to face it-painful as it is.
He is off his rocker.
I fear so.
Most of all-he told me-he dreads-
Her constant, 'watching',
"Her eyes-those huge, blue eyes-
Are everywhere! They follow me! They follow!
There's nowhere, nowhere,
I can hide, from her!"
He has told me-looking truly desperate.
I commiserated. Or tried to.
But what does one say?
He fears her-'retribution'.
And he believes-ridiculously enough-
That she put a curse, on him.

Apocryphal or true-
I leave it up to you!

I for one-go my way,
Having learned enough-
And far more than I ever first wanted to-
On this strange and most elusive, refractory subject.
Let others, ponder-another day.

I leave it now to
Other hands, other cognitions, other eyes.
Those with a fresh perspective-
And open minds.
Those with a pristine, clear,
And un-jaded curiosity.
And-particularly-
Those so blissfully unaware,
Of the very real dangers involved.

Yes, I say,
Let others ponder.
I wish to enjoy,
What remains of my retirement-
In peace.
In my beautiful, old Georgetown house.
With my pipe and slippers,
My five, lovely, daughters.
Nine, beautiful, grandchildren,
Visiting, me often.

My books, music, sports,
Interests, walks, cronies, old movies,
Old television shows,
Academic and historical studies-
For alas-I lost my dear and beloved wife,
Nine years ago.

I spend my time nowadays-
Mostly reflecting-
On the past-mine and the world's-
As befits an old, cold warrior-such as I.
But-I leave it to others.
For I have spent quite long
Enough, in the shadows-thank you!

Perhaps, I'm getting too old
For this sort of thing.
Perhaps not.
Anyway-
I bequeath it.
Let others ponder.

Let the truth come out-
For truth is the breath of life.
It may be soon, it may be yonder.
But it will happen,
One day...

Her name is Brigit Keller,
A middle aged woman, a fortune teller,
Is she only a clairvoyant,
Advising her wealthy clients,
Or is she a dweller,
In a dark, unseen and hidden world?
I cannot speak.
I cannot tell.
I cannot know.
Can you?

July 14   2011   9.2-9-14.p.m.

FOR THE WORLD

Sing for the world,
And bring for the word,
All the joy you possess!

Fight for the world,
But light for the world,
Candles for those in distress.

Reach for the world,
Yet teach for the world,
That hope can-make a way.

Think for the world,
And drink for the world,
The cup of beauty every day!

Be bold, for the world,
Then hold for the world,
Each ounce of love-you can find.

Take for the world,
Yet make for the world,
Every wonder-in your mind.

Give for the world,
Live for the world,
The dreams-you dream-of peace.

Drive for the world,
And strive, for the world,
Until the evils-cease.

Plea for the world,
And free for the world,
Until-your victory-you win!

Strong for the world,
But-wrong, for the world-
The path that leads to sin.

Cry for the world-
Sigh for the world,
That chooses evil over good.

Pray for the world-
Say for the world-
They each did-what they could.

Nicholas Alexander Papantoniou

October 28 1989   7.-7.11.p.m

NIGHTMARE ANGEL

I had a nightmare, a heavy nightmare,
That blood was dripping, while I was tripping,
On stones, high, drip, drip from the sockets
Of some innocent man's, departed eyes.
So be thankful for holy tears and your sweat
Was like acid to my fingers, in the darkness.
While the sun came through the door.
And there-in the doorway-beckoned an angel.

And in a strange way, I thought, 'hey',
This is the thing, the clandestine, crappy thing
In which the poor skeletons of death fall apart
On the floor and I leave you alone my beloved
No more and we fly into the blank,
Face of time tonight.
For I'm free to know you with
Wonder and purity my love.

The sunbeams, of some dreams, or one dreams.
And the moonbeams, of soon beams, or boon dreams.
The star beams, of our dreams, or far dreams.
Approach you and cast off your fear and your lies
And step into the death, of the mad bag, of phoney
Lived life and beyond to the great door of infinity-
Open to you now, a few eternal steps ahead.
So follow my lead and I'll follow your path,
Like two eagles, soaring high through a rainbow!

Like a wave of water, I almost caught her,
That elusive daughter, of divine Godly,
High and sun-dry glory-that blistered my hands.
So welcome, the hard or easy way forward.
In the past, in the dark, a slime dripping tunnel
Of torment, that led to a tunnel of love and brought
Me to your arms, far above my fears or dreams of
Wonderful womanhood, I ever wanted.

In a cave of despair, I could save-if I care-
The souls of all who quit in the filth,
Of maggots, that crawl, luminous, writhing and rotten,
In which there is no bottom, once you plunge
Through the floor and how their blood spurted high,
14,000 miles in the sky and I dreamed of a place

Where I saw things blossoming.

But the stench turned foul and I rode through
The dark, that was very dimly lit and I strode
And climbed-waist deep in gore.
Daring, dank, adoring, un-dwindled in knowledge
Of the devious, dooming distance, detached from all
That I hear and see and smell. Into the fate-
Floating, fleeting, fluttering, fawn-like over the heads,
Of the lost beings and several, subterranean,
Supernatural-splintered souls.
In a vortex of perpetual, anguish.

And now I thought, 'wow', if I can swim and dance
And turn and spin and lunge and score and strike
And smash and stretch my way through this twisting sand
Of foul vomit-veering, valiantly up,
Then tomorrow, is not wasted yet and soon will come
The day when air is sweet and pure to the taste again.
And love can save the world. Not lost and abandoned
As my love's eyes, gazed, into and beyond,
The deep, whole, hole of evil.

So I rose and I climbed through the tribulations of struggle,
And I span and swerved and swivelled
And swooped and swirled
And scored and struck and smashed and stood
And the stench turned clear
And light and I broke out
And I was free.

November 4   2009   8.1.-9.29.p.m.

IT'S ME

Listen, listen,
To the sound of the axe!
Chop, chop, chop, chop.
A testament, that all things drop.
The final squeeze, of breath, the final pop.
The final stride, for some-a limp or crawl or hop.
Chop, chop, chop, chop, chop.
Ah yes!
Often, have I heard it.

Now, listen, listen,
To the noise of the hammer!
Bam, bam, bam, bam.
A sweet drought, a precious dram!
For Pete or Bill or John or George or Sam.
For one of great importance,
Or one not worth a dam.
Bam, bam, bam, bam, bam.
I like to hear it. I really do.

Listen, to the tune of the sword.
Cling, cling, cling, cling.
How sweetly, does it sing!
What happy memories, does it bring.
What sudden changes, does it ring.
Cling, cling, cling, cling, cling.
It is nice music to my ears!

Yet, listen, to the echo of the guns!
Boom, boom, boom, boom.
Each a report, of a personal doom.
Each a lesson, in individual gloom.
Each a last chapter in a book-
Of I know not whom.
Boom, boom, boom, boom, boom.
It's quite a relaxing sound, I think!

So listen to the strain of the scream.
Eek! Eek! Eek! Eek!
What solace, what succour-does it seek?
For the bold, the brave, the coward or the meek.
The beautiful flower of hope-
Now, it does rot and shrivel, droop and reek.

Eek! Eek! Eek! Eek! Eek!
What a pleasant, sound!

Oh, listen, to the muffle of the weeping.
Sob, sob, sob, sob.
How they weep-for those that save,
Or those that rob.
For Harry or Terry or Jim or Dick or Bob.
For the greatest fop, or the greatest slob.
Sob, sob, sob, sob, sob.
So many, many times, I've heard it!

Then, listen to the peal of the bells.
Clang, clang, clang, clang.
How truly beautifully it rang.
How wonderfully, nobly it sang!
For those that die heroes,
Or those that hang.
Clang, clang, clang, clang, clang.
What a charming, sound!

Ah, now listen, to the cadence of the spade.
Chunk, chunk, chunk, chunk.
How, the once happy hearts, have sunk!
For soldier, sailor, rich man, poor man,
Beggar man, nun or monk.
Chunk, chunk, chunk, chunk, chunk.
I like to hear the noise, I truly do.

Listen to the hush of the prayer.
Blah, blah, blah, blah, blah.
The noise is soft,
It does not carry far,
It does not much,
The mellow evening mar.
Whether in peace, or whether in war.
Blah, blah, blah, blah.
It matters not, to me!

Yes, of course-it's me!
As you who read this-
Man or woman, young or old or neither-
Will, one day, find out.
I'm waiting for you.
For you and him
And her and she and he,
And they and those and all, all, all others.

I'm very fair. Very discreet. Very polite.
Very impartial.
I take no sides. I play no favourites.
Hush-hush-is the the word.
(That's the secret of my success.)
I will wait very patiently for you.
No rush. No fuss. No worry. No bother.
No doubt.
Be calm. All will be well.
I'm rather good at this,
If I may say so, myself.
Just, take my hand-
When the time comes-
I'll, lead the way!

I know my business,
And I work with a quiet hum.
For I have had much practice,
And much to come!

Don't concern yourself about it,
Leave it to me.
For I await the great pleasure,
Of your company!

For I am death.
The enemy of life,
The victor of it too-
Though-some-I know-
Do question that.

For-I am the grim reaper,
I am the eternal keeper,
And-you-the immortal sleeper,
I seek!

From, the beginning of time,
Till the end,
It's a journey,
We both wend,
It is for me to send-you-
To the great abyss!

It is my-not your-realm,
It is I-not life-at the helm,
And I will, overwhelm,
Every, every, every living thing-

In time.

You do not have to ask,
For it is my solemn, happy task,
Then drink, drink, drink deep of the flask,
Of life-
Be it, long or short!
(While you still can.)

The brave man, the noble man,
The foolish man, the geek,
Are all equally mine, to claim,
One to my eyes-that seek,
Only your comfort
And peace and repose-
Forevermore.

I want to help you!
Truly I do.
For isn't life a very heavy load?
Haven't you trudged, long enough-
Upon that weary, dreary, teary-unjust-unfair road?
I have compassion, sympathy, empathy.
It's a part of my code.
But-know that-I must reap,
What you have sowed,
So, do be very careful
What you sow!

All, those sounds.
Oh, those sounds!
Are beautiful to me!
A lovely signal.
An old fashioned, calling card.
A wonderful doorbell-to my world.
They fill me, with laughter and joy,
And happiness and peace and merriment,
So sweetly!

Some say, I'm a towering figure,
Dressed in white, with a hood-
And in my hand, a giant scythe.
The implacable, enemy,
Of all things alive.
But my work is so soothing to me,
And my-how it does thrive!

I am very reasonable.
Very flexible.
I am not impatient.
I am not hasty.
It will not be a rush job.
I promise.
I can wait.

I have done this work for millennia,
For ages and ages and aeons,
But my work is still so fresh to me!
I know my timeless, ways, so well, you see!
I have no favourites.
You are all my favourites!
All. All.
All of you!

I come,
Not to judge,
To praise, to condemn, or malign
Nor reward, nor punish
But to close. To shut. To finish.
Close the book.
That final, appointment.
That finishing, rendezvous.
That last bass-voiced call to the still-living.
That late, late show.
The termination. Conclusion,
Call it what you will-
The game is over.
It's up.
We both know it.
We do!
I am your utter-completion.

And you-who are reading this, right now-
Yes-I can see you.
Your time-will come, too.
It really matters not when.
In an hour, a day, a week, a month,
A year, a decade, a century.
I will be calmly, serenely,
Tranquilly, coolly, waiting.
And then-
But, why go into that now?
It is a lovely, lovely day, isn't it?

Enjoy it.

So I care not.
I care not.
I care not at all!
Not at all.
I have time.
Absolutely, endless,
Limitless time.
And I am looking forward,
To seeing you-
One day-
Again.

August 27   2011 3.05-4.55.a.m

MABEL, GABLE AND THE TABLE

Here, I-a local man-a janitor-
Do tell the strange story of
Mabel, Gable and the table.

Tall Tom Gable and blonde
Miss Mabel Macready,
Were found dead,
In an empty log cabin, in Vermont.
Both lying on a huge oak table.
Nothing more.

The cabin was quite empty-
Save for the table,
The door was wide open.
No cars were outside.
They were both respectably
And properly attired.
There were no signs of struggle.
Mabel-had been strangled.
The table was brand new and spotless clean.
Like a mirror.
No chairs. No other furniture at all.
The doctors could not precisely determine
The cause of Gable's death.

It was one of the great unsolved
Mysteries of the locality.
Everybody talked about it.
Everyone knew all the details, real well.
Not that there were any details to speak of-
You see, so it was pretty easy to remember.
Everyone was a-scratching their heads,
Over it-for the longest time.

Now-it wasn't a bear-
In case you were thinking that.
They ruled that out-right off.
There were no signs, hairs, furs, furry forensics,
Saliva, paw, jaw, or claw prints-and no blood.
And a huge bear couldn't go around on tip-toe-
Leaving no clues-no evidence-
No trace-no disturbance-you see-
So-it was no bear.

The foul deed stood out,
Like a spire or a gable,
On a roof of iniquitous sin,
In an empty, rickety, spooky old house,
That no one had ever lived in.

No one high or low,
Wise or dumb,
Quick or slow,
Has ever solved-
Or could begin to plumb,
The strange mystery of
Gable, Mabel, the table.

Gable?
Tom Gable was a weird man,
So it was believed, anyways.
Certainly, he was a strange one.
Some folks said he had
Worked once in a chemist,
Others said he had worked one time
In a race track stable.
No one knows too much-you see-
About big, bad and maybe mad-
Tom Gable.

It was said he passionately
Loved, Mabel Macready.
A blue eyed, beauty-
Of twenty three.
Who spurned his love.
So did this enable-
Tom to strangle Mabel,
With a rope or a cable?
Well, no.
For no tools were used-
Save his own bare hands.

Men would marvel at the beauty
Of sexy, doe-eyed Mabel.
They said she looked a little like
Marilyn Monroe-or maybe-Betty Grable.
Alas, she ended up on an oak table.
Murdered by Tom Gable.

A tall, red haired,
Brown eyed, pale faced man.
With frightening, wild eyes.
Oh, they lay it on with a ladle.
When telling creepy deeds
And far-out stuff,
Of spectacularly sinister,
Solitary, Mr Tom Gable.

A man-this much is known-of about thirty two.
Freakishly strong and powerful.
A mighty tree chopper-or a lumberjack.
A grip like a vice. Real quick-for his size.
He could handle a chainsaw-
Like you and me use a fork.
His voice-a growling baritone.
Not an ounce of fat, on his
Statuesque frame.

Six feet four-that's for sure-
Some say-at least a good inch-
Or-maybe two more.
Shoulders like a barn door.
Huge feet, long arms, long legs,
And huge, big knuckled, alabaster hands.
More than able,
To strangle a poor, sweet, kind, helpless girl,
Like unfortunate Mabel.

Some liked him.
Some found him insufferable.
Nobody knew where
He came from originally-
Nor anything he done prior
To showing up here.
He just fetched up in these parts-
A few years ago-
Won about a dozen arm wrestling
Contests in bars-done it easy too.
Saw him do it, myself.
Some folks say-and I believe them-
That he was just about strong enough
To have been a professional strongman.
Where he came from?
I'll fess up-nobody hardly wanted to ask him.

People were put off-
By his intimidating,
Formidable appearance
And unsociable disposition.
He always appeared to be
Sort of contemplative, thoughtful,
Ruminating, deliberating, brooding.
And just a little bit pissed off.
Didn't say too much.
Man of few words.
Strong, silent type.
Still waters-run deep.
Oh, all them clichés,
Came out pretty easy-
A lonely, lost alpha male.
Maybe-ex-military,
Ex-Marine type-sure looked it.
Ultra-right wing feller.
Ultra-left wing guy.
Maybe-one of them green-freaks-you know-
A veggie-terrorist.
People had suspicions-by the barrel load.
But nobody knew zip for sure!
Those weird, frightening, squinting eyes-
Turning on you-
Lurking behind thick, reddish-brown,
Bushy eyebrows.
Like a wild, hungry, ornery animal,
A-watching you-closely-
From under the branches of a tree-
As you walk along by.

Some people figured
He had a dark, peculiar, dangerous-
Mysterious-maybe even-a secret past-
And that was why
He always looked so pissed.

Since the real facts were unavailable,
Many have invented others.
The details divided,
Sisters and brothers,
Fathers and Mothers,
Sweethearts and lovers,
In polite dispute.
The speculation covers-
The local territory.

And all this conjecture-
Obscures and smothers-
The exact truth-whatever it may be-
In the strange, anomalous
And tragic tale of
Mabel, Gable and the
Brand new, oak table.

It makes no more sense
Than the tower of Babel!
It is a fathomless enigma,
No one can hurdle or climb or straddle.
And it will surely-scramble, tangle or addle,
The brain cells-of anyone who
Would presume or dare to paddle-
In the deep, dark waters
Of wonder and weirdness.
The silent, sphinx-like enigma-lingers-
Of Mabel and Gable and the table.

And the reporters, writers,
Investigators, detectives, journalists-come and go.
For some-most welcome-for others-intolerable.
Curiosity-seekers, hard-core, homicide-likers,
And murder groupies.
Lovers of strangulation-hippie hikers.
Weekend Satanists-passing through-
And neo-Nazi, bikers.
Serious skiers and half-assed pikers.
All the trash and rabble,
Skittle and scuttle and slip and scrabble and grapple,
Trying to work out the curious conundrum,
Of the table, Mabel and Gable.

Some said of Tom Gable,
That he was very jealous of flirty Mabel,
And thus killed her on the table.
And then died of a broken heart.
Others say, he did not.

Others said he studied,
The arcane philosophy of Zabel.
And that motivated him to kill Mabel.
Others say, he did not.

Others say-early on that fateful morning-
He breakfasted at a favourite drive-in restaurant.

On a big, fat stack of hot buckwheat pancakes-
Smothered with butter and the syrup of maple,
The juice of an apple,
And six eggs.
Fried onions, mushrooms,
Peppers and tomatoes, cheese
And sausages-for this was his staple.
And this gave him indigestion and anger,
To kill poor Mabel.
Others say, he did not.

Some say he did cradle,
Dying Mabel-gently-in his arms,
With a broken heart.
And then expired himself,
Mysteriously-inexplicably.
For reasons totally unknown.
Others say, he did not.

Some say he did dabble,
In the dark arts.
Went to a séance-or two-
Maybe-just out of curiosity-
That spooked him out real bad-
And then-the devil-maybe-made him to do it.
And all this twisted-turned his sick,
Ailing, diseased mind-
Into killing pure, innocent Mabel.
Others say, he did not.

Some say he was,
Abducted by aliens,
One night-alone-in the woods-
Taken to another planet-
Experimented on fiendishly-
Brought back-brainwashed-
And told to forget all about his abduction.
And this explains his sudden madness
And real strange behaviour.
Others say, he was not.

Some say he was,
A serial killer.
With dozens of victims, young and old,
All buried out in the woods,
All chopped up, nice and regular.
Others say, he was not.

Was he even capable of pity?
Was he ever-indeed-real rational?
Or was he quite unstable?
Before he killed Mabel, on the table?

There are stories,
That he hated beautiful women,
For their ceaseless, teasing.
And that he had killed many men,
In ways less than pleasing.
That he strangled-with his huge, pale hands-
Several Wall Street bankers,
And he called it; 'Quantitative easing.'

There are rumours,
That he was a part time Satanist.

There are rumours,
That he was a weekend neo-Nazi.

There are rumours,
That he was a communist.

Oh, there are such stories!
But each of them,
Was believed to be,
Just another, dumb fable,
Had nothing to do with Mable,
And was nowhere near the table.
Another monstrous, dippy tale,
Told of fierce, towering, lonely,
Glowering, terrible Tom Gable.

One woman,
The local Irish fortune reader,
Mary O'Flint-
Said that Gable didn't kill Mabel at all.
Uh-uh. No way. Not a chance!
Them bad things-people say, he done-
He never done them.
That's just what she said.
She said, Gable, wasn't a bad man,
Just misunderstood.
He was a good man-deep down.
He done excellent things-in his time-she reckoned.
But got overtook bad-by circumstances.

Covered up, his shy, gentle, kind,
Introverted and sensitive soul,
With a fake mask of aggression and hostility.
She said, he learned how to do that at school, from being
Constantly picked on-
Having people always finding fault-
And never finding no love nor encouragement.
She said-he was eccentric-but-very clean cut.
Sure-he was a loner or a recluse or a hermit-
But that don't make you a killer-and he didn't do it.
A stranger done it-and then took off into
The wide woods-just as he saw Gable arriving.
Leaving Mabel, dead, on the table.
Then Gabel found Mabel on the table.
And died of pure grief-himself-
Was just inconsolable.
So much real love had he-for she.
And that-though he didn't have a ring on him
(They searched him, of course.)
Gable was planning to propose marriage
To Mabel-real soon-that's for sure-perhaps even-
On the very day that he found her lying
Dead, on the oak table.
She said that the table was there,
For some weirdo kind of ceremony.

Now, this could all be true.
Some do believe it.
And believe it most religiously.
But on the whole-Mary O'Flint-
Who likes the occasional drink-
Shall we say-
Didn't get too many takers.

Mabel?
Real popular!
This is a small but friendly town.
Lots of people knew her.
Knew lots and lots of stuff about her.
Oh, she was plenty popular
Around these parts!
But what happened to her
Was just about unthinkable.
That's just exactly-
What most folks said about her awful sad death.
Everybody talked about her-after she was gone.
Still do-I reckon.

She was the kind of gal that
Leaves quite an impression-you know?
There wasn't one person in this town,
Could say a single, solitary bad word about her,
And-mind you-they knew everything-she ever done.
She was said-by those that always
Knew her best-to have had a sweet, kind,
Almost dove-like disposition.
Just an all-American angel-they said.
Was a good, honest Christian soul.
Always, fought the good fight.
Went to church, Sundays.
Where in the choir-she would warble.
She had a soft, gentle, innocent heart.
Liked to dance.
Liked to laugh.
Liked to live.
Was nice and considerate and sweet
And polite and kind to just everyone-
Young and old, rich and poor-
Regardless of their ethnicity,
Race or religion or life-style.
Which is more than I could say for some around here.
Was modest, optimistic, naive.
A girl with a real good, solid,
Wholesome, moral disposition.
Used to give money to charities-regular-
Even though she wasn't any too wealthy, herself.
Left school when she was fourteen.
She had just a lovely smile-
Like concentrated sunshine.
Lovely, pearly white teeth.
A lovely, high-pitched voice.
A lovely, smooth, pink complexion.
A lovely figure-slim, petite,
But very curvy, very busty.
A lovely, cute, shapely rear, too.
Sure-plenty of men in this town-
Had a thing for her-I guess-
Wouldn't hardly be human-if they didn't!
Her girlishness was incomparable.
About five feet two inches.
Had big, innocent, childlike,
Trusting, blue eyes.
Had a lovely cute, little, turned up nose.
Long, blonde hair.
Her beauty-was just delectable.

Wore a double, 'D', cup brassier.
Worked as a check-out girl.
Used to write sad poetry.
Liked to like to sing, as she done the gardening.
Liked to read, sappy romance novels.
Liked going to the movies.
Liked burgers, steaks,
Done rare-with lots of raw onions.
Frankfurters, bratwurst-with sauerkraut-
And lots of mustard.
And vanilla ice cream-with lots of nuts
Or lots of cinnamon-peanut butter-apple pie.
And real thick, chocolate milkshakes!
Liked fresh squeezed orange juice-for breakfast.
Liked pop music and also all furry animals.
Chewed bubble gum a lot.
Drank diet coke.
Still read comic books.
Wouldn't hurt a fly.
Warmed-at first-to shy,
Lonely, Tom Gable.
She often wore pretty short skirts,
High heels. Lots of make-up-
(Which she didn't need.)
Wore tight T-shirts, real tight blue jeans.
And sometimes wore a coat of sable.
Wanted to be an actress-
Or even a movie star.
Took long walks in the woods-
But never really-went too far!
Had just bought her own car.
Sometimes-she didn't even-
Bother to wear a bra-
But this was just a rumour,
Like so very many others,
In the real odd case of
Mabel, Gable, table.

The table?
Oh, it was about nine feet long.
About four feet wide.
Fine, beautiful piece of wood.
Polished. Smooth. Shiny. Inscrutable.
Brand new, real thick. Darned heavy.
Nobody knew who bought it.
Gable didn't. Mabel didn't.
The authorities checked.

Nicholas Alexander Papantoniou

Its mystery was intractable.
Anyway, turns out-
The cabin belonged to an old retired feller-
Who let Gable, use it for hunting.
This much is incontrovertible.
But the cabin-was brand new-built-
Just about a year, before the fatal incident.
And had no previous furniture-at all.
The old feller it belonged to didn't
Buy the table and said he didn't know
Nothing at all about no dang table.
So nobody knew how it got there.
Or who put it there.
Or who got it through
The narrow cabin door.
Or was it built in the cabin?
If so-how? By who? And why? When?
Its presence was insoluble.

It was all most peculiar and strange.
Many a beer has been downed
In bars over the years-by our local guys,
And many a coffee too-
In private homes by our local ladies,
All just speculating-
On the whole darn, mysterious thing.

In beautiful Vermont,
It will always be, ineluctably,
A romantic, mystery.

Bringing plenty of tourists and trade,
Plenty of players and plenty of played,
And will the memory ever fade?
Murder enthusiasts-have it made,
And true believers-won't be swayed.

Local folk, sigh.
Oh my.
For beautiful, lost, sweet, young Mabel.
For strange, sad Gable.
And the unsolved riddle,
Of the shiny, polished table.

In confusion and misinformation
And disinformation and-even-piss-information,
The case is forever swaddled.

You cannot walk through the facts-
You just have to waddle.
There are no facts, (hardly any at all),
You see-to walk through.

But, after all-what else can I say?
There's no need to label.
It was just Mabel, Gabel and a table.
That's all.